THE BONES OF TIME

Liliane

"Now I was alone with her and did not know what to do. She let me take her small hand and led us to La Capéranie, her home, protesting all the while that I walked too fast for her short legs. I tried to slow down. I had no idea how to communicate with such a young child. Fortunately, she took the initiative and started talking . . ."

Liliane Richman brings her artistic genius to the familial separation and life-altering hardships thrust on Europeans during WWII—most vividly in the account of her father's first grasp.

—Deborah Reardon,
Amazon best-selling author of *Blue Suede Shoes*

THE
BONES
OF
TIME

LILIANE RICHMAN

THE BONES OF TIME

Copyright © 2016 Liliane Richman

All rights reserved. No part of this publication may be reproduced, stored in any retrieval system, or transmitted in any form or by any means, mechanical, photocopying, recording, or otherwise, without permission in writing from the publisher, except by a reviewer, who may quote brief passages in a review.

Cover and Interior design by Ted Ruybal
Manufactured in the United States of America

For more information, please contact:

Wisdom House Books
www.wisdomhousebooks.com

Paperback ISBN 13: 978-0-9966356-0-8
LCCN: 2016902144

HIS016000 HISTORY / Historiography
HIS043000 HISTORY / Holocaust
HIS022000 HISTORY / Jewish
1 2 3 4 5 6 7 8 9 10

www.thebonesoftime.com

In the Heart of Ferns

*In the heart of my childhood
in the forest of ferns
so long ago a village mine
there is a place
the iris of my eye*

*Inside the grandmother reads
the Three Musketeers
with a magnifying glass
while her daughter beats the garden path
left and right watching out for snakes*

*Her husband who loves carpentry better than his own job
fashions chairs wheelbarrows
tables and clogs
then pedals his bicycle to work
sitting straight back
a king on his throne*

When he comes home
he gazes at trees
as if they were the sea
what does he see?

I ask
can I come back when I'm old?
say twenty-three with my babies?
he smiles
Silly, you won't want to when you're 23

Now they're all gone
the grandmother the father the mother
I search their house the garage the garden
with summer geraniums
there's no one
least of all me
their adopted child
in the ferns that keep on growing

Table of Contents

Prologue	ix
Part 1: EUGÈNE & CARMEN	**1**
Chapter 1	3
Chapter 2	9
Chapter 3	17
Chapter 4	25
Chapter 5	29
Chapter 6	33
Chapter 7	39
Chapter 8	43
Chapter 9	55
Chapter 10	63
Chapter 11	71
Chapter 12	75
Chapter 13	81
Chapter 14	87
Chapter 15	95
Chapter 16	107
Chapter 17	111

Chapter 18 117

Chapter 19 125

Chapter 20 129

Chapter 21 133

Part 2: LILIANE **145**

Chapter 22 147

Chapter 23 151

Chapter 24 155

Chapter 25 159

Chapter 26 169

Chapter 27 175

Chapter 28 185

Chapter 29 191

Chapter 30 195

Chapter 31 201

Chapter 32 205

Chapter 33 215

Chapter 34 221

Chapter 35 229

Epilogue 233

A Tour Through The Gardens 235

Acknowledgements 243

Prologue

It was my brother Fred who gave me the incentive to write this story, not in so many words, but by an osmosis through which we communicated at times. Indeed, Fred and I shared a meta-language related to our mostly unspoken but close awareness of each other, of our childhood shadowed by war, the effects of which we carry in our bones.

Fred, his wife Jeanette, and I were traveling from Paris to Annecy to visit their son Alex and his family. Jeanette and I had been chatting, catching up on events, as people do when they live far apart and reunite again.

From the corner of my eye I observed Fred quietly pulling a book out of his luggage. Always interested in what anyone reads, I glanced at the title and was surprised.

"*Grimm's Fairy Tales?*" I exclaimed. "Strange reading them at your age!"

"Not so strange," Fred replied. "There was this kid I met at school when we lived in Sabres who spoke about the Brothers Grimm's fairy tales all the time. He said they were spooky and sometimes bloody; they gave him nightmares, but he loved them anyway. Of course, he was an ordinary boy living with two parents, secure in his home in the village of his birth. I was too busy with my own nightmares to read scary tales."

Fear can be thrilling when you feel safe.

"Yes, but why this sudden interest in fairy tales?" I asked.

"Curiosity, to see what they are about. And look, I've found an interesting one. It's a tale about a father and his four sons, one of whom meets a tailor. I think you could write something about that."

Of course I caught his drift; our father was a tailor. It seemed an odd request, but it flattered me that my brother believed in my writing. I answered, "Perhaps," and forgot all about it until the day I lost Fred forever.

Shortly thereafter, and still aggrieved over Fred's untimely passing, I remembered the Annecy voyage and his suggestion. Now I was eager to write a memoir about our family, to preserve our experiences and extraordinary survival during a chaotic period of history.

A poor man had four sons. When they were grown, he sent them out into the world to acquire a profession. The fourth son met a tailor. "How would you like to be my apprentice?" he asked the young man. And when the young man's training was completed, his master gave him a needle. "With this needle," he said, "there will be nothing in the world you won't know how to sew or repair."

-From the Grimm tale of "The Four Brothers"

Part One

EUGÈNE & CARMEN

Chapter One

When my father, Eugène, was a boy, Hungary was a backward country. Life in a metropolis like Budapest might well be transformed by the arrival of modern amenities such as electricity, running water, and movie theaters. No such improvements reached the slumbering village of Tyukod. The children talked constantly about automobiles, radios, and airplanes, though they had never seen any of these wonders. They rather believed them to be fairy tales, fantasies much like the unicorns and dragons of the past.

For the approximately one thousand souls who lived in Tyukod, these novelties were so far out of reach that even the local wealthy man, Count Ozwat, continued traveling through the countryside on horseback, well after my father left home to be apprenticed in a distant village, even after he returned to bid goodbye to his parents, and right before his departure for France.

Eugène's family, one of a dozen Jewish families who lived in Tyukod, had never experienced anything exotic in their lives. They were too busy to waste time dreaming about such things. They knew apples, but neither bananas nor oranges. They talked about the cow and about his father's occasional shoe repair business. They debated the slaughtering of a goose for the New Year celebration, and whether or not the crop of cabbage, made into sauerkraut, a staple of their daily meals, would suffice to feed them for the entire winter. In truth, outside of occasional quarreling between the brothers, there was no time for much other conversation at home. Except for his father's prayer books, there were no books in their home. His mother, dear soul, didn't know how to read; besides, reading materials such as novels and magazines had to be obtained in the city. Those precious few schoolbooks Eugène learned from remained at school overnight. He didn't know what a bedtime story was.

What he did remember most warmly about his childhood home life centered around his mother, Fanny. She worked from sunup to sunset, day in and day out, making everything they ate or wore. Whatever the weather, in the cold of winter or the heat of summer, she was always up before anyone else. She washed, ironed, knitted sweaters and scarves, stuffed pillows with goose down, milked the cow, churned the cream into butter, and warmed the sauerkraut extracted from huge barrels for winter meals. She prepared apple and plum preserves, canned the tomatoes, kneaded dough for challah, and shaped noodles that looked like butterflies with a fast twisting movement of her hands. She brightened their weekly Sabbath with the wonderful nutty cheesecake they ate, along with warm gulps of tea made with the mint that grew in wild patches in the garden.

There was a butcher shop in the village, though beef was too expensive an item for the family's table; and of course, they ate no pork. But they had a few chickens and some geese. The latter force-fed until their livers grew disproportionately. Eugène's mother sold the geese to a traveling middleman who came to the village to collect

PART ONE—EUGÈNE & CARMEN
CHAPTER ONE

them. He, in turn, sold them to French producers who transformed them into *foie gras*. Such delicacies would never reach the family's table, but with the proceeds of these sales, Fanny bought more goslings and the fattening process began anew. The profits she made went to the exceptional purchase of new pants or a shirt for her husband, a struggling shoemaker. The rest of the family wore hand-me-downs altered by Fanny's weary needle.

Years later Eugène could still smell the odor of his mother's confections and the taste of the cream and cheeses she prepared. He never tired of watching her cook. He was an acknowledged gourmand and cleaned her pots and pans with his little finger or, when her back was turned, with his tongue. He knew all her gestures and replicated the motion of her fingers as she prepared her sweet-and-sour cabbage. The palm of her hand swiftly shaped the meat while her agile fingers folded the cabbage leaf around it. The rolled-up leaves simmered for an hour and a half while emitting a most divine odor. The taste of a savory memory! When he recalled those times, he still saw himself sitting at the kitchen table, warm and happy to be alive in the simple world that was his until he turned twelve.

The Gentile children in Tyukod were, for the most part, as poor as the Jewish families who resided there. Eugène would have gladly played with any one of them. But for some reason he did not understand, they chased after him and called him and his family "Christ killers."

He felt confused and protested vehemently, told them he didn't know this Christ person. He had never been a visitor to Eugène's home. In fact, they hardly ever had any guests, except for his mother's family, who came to celebrate the Jewish High Holidays with them.

No, he was certain he hadn't met any man bearing the name Christ, and even if he had, he would not have wanted to kill him, or anyone else for that matter. The idea of spilled blood was abhorrent to him; the thought of it made his stomach queasy. Eugène hated it when his mother bled the geese or the chickens. He knew he should never kill anyone, unless perhaps as the result of dire threat, for self-defense. Even then, the very idea sent a chill down his spine. He was kind of a weakling anyway, too scared to throw a stone at a mouse. For protection he stuck close to his older brother, Elias, who came to pick him up at school when he had time. Elias was a stocky young man with a booming voice, the self-appointed protector of the twenty or so Jewish children who attended the village's one-room schoolhouse.

When Eugène turned thirteen, during his last year of school, his parents and some of the other Jewish families in Tyukod hired an itinerant rabbi to instruct their sons in preparations for their Bar Mitzvahs, the ceremony that turns a thirteen-year-old boy into a responsible member of the Jewish community. They were to memorize and chant passages from the Old Testament in Hebrew, to Eugène an alien tongue with rough sounds that hurt his throat. The boys repeated the strange words and sentences they heard over and over again. Eugène ventured to ask Rabbi Zukor what they all meant.

"Don't worry about that, Iene. Just repeat what I say," he replied.

And his own father, Samuel, who prayed each morning in a similar hurried, unintelligible manner, patted his head and reiterated, "Do like he says, my son."

Thus, not understanding what he was forced to repeat, he never developed a relationship with God and became an atheist before he knew what that word meant.

PART ONE—EUGÈNE & CARMEN
CHAPTER ONE

Elias was nine years older than Eugène when he became the head of the family during World War I. He had no skills other than bartering, buying, and reselling cigarettes, liquor, or any product in demand that he could turn into profit to help feed the family after their father was sent to the front.

His father's prolonged absence during this time perhaps explains why Eugène remembered so little about him. He was a sickly man when he returned after four years of the murderous conflict. Always a quiet man, Samuel became even more so. His lungs had been damaged by the mustard gas he breathed in the trenches. Though a veteran of the Hungarian army, twenty-six years later, already in his late sixties, nearly blind and deaf, he would be rounded up by Eichmann and his Hungarian allies, who sent him to be gassed in a crematorium in Auschwitz.

Elias, thrust into the turmoil and hardships brought on by World War I, took to traveling farther and farther, close to the borders into Romania and Yugoslavia, sometimes as far as Poland. There he acquired cheap goods of all kinds and resold them at a profit.

After his father's return, and against his wishes, Elias continued selling contraband. He had nearly been caught by the local police and, for safety's sake, escaped all the way to Budapest. There he met up with like-minded people, those who wished to earn easy money and have some fun with the rest of their time. He found a respectable salesman's job in a lady's hat shop, or so he told his parents, with whom he maintained sporadic contact.

In the meantime, Zelman, the second brother, quit school to work for a grocer in a nearby village. Now it was Eugène's turn to seek employment of some kind. His formal education came to an abrupt end. He would never become a carefree teenager. Instead, like most boys he grew up with, he would have to learn a trade and help his parents with his wages. Thus, he became apprenticed to a master tailor in the town of Szeged, over two hundred kilometers away. Was he sad to leave home? He couldn't remember his feelings. After all, he was still an ignorant child without ambitions or aspirations of his own. All he knew for sure was that life was not easy for his family.

Later, when he began reading their history, the history of Hungarian Jews, Eugène discovered that his ancestors were used to hurried departures, sometimes in much harsher circumstances than his own. Consequently, they learned not to wax sentimental about places and things. Often they left with nothing more than the knowledge and the creativity stored in their brains. Over time they settled the world over, even as far as China and Patagonia. Eugène, as well, carried that weightless, wandering gene that had ensured his people's precarious survival throughout the centuries. Because of this he did not get attached to material possessions, had no use for bric-a-brac or for anything unessential to the sustenance of life, to his family's chagrin much later.

When he was in his late eighties, and had plenty of time to reconsider the course of his life, Eugène questioned and wondered why a thirteen-year-old child should be sent to live so far away from his family. Had his father sat him down and explained the necessity of his going away, he might not have felt such a lingering sense of abandonment so many years thereafter.

Chapter Two

Eugène's boss was a nice enough man, a master who taught him to thread his needle like lightning, with a single movement of his hand. He drove it through the cloth, a gesture he practiced endlessly for the first six months of his apprenticeship until he acquired a smooth, unbroken rhythm. He grew accustomed to the soft and steady susurration caused by the contact of needle on cloth; the lullaby of a tailor's trade, the cachet of sartorial genius. During the course of the next five years, because he was obedient and wanted to please, he learned to hem carefully so the stitches stayed invisible on either side of the cloth.

"With such a needle, mark my words," commented his master, Mr. Feldman, "there's nothing in the world you won't be able to fix."

Eugène became adept at the sewing machine and learned to take a client's measurements. The next steps were drafting patterns on paper with tailor's chalk and learning to transfer the pattern onto the cloth. He first applied the process to a pair of pants. The remaining endeavor, and the most difficult for a beginner to accomplish, was making the jacket, complete with its lining. Ten hours a day, six days a week, constituted backbreaking work. He lived for Sundays and summer evenings when he and the other two apprentices played soccer in the grassy field behind the post office until the sky darkened.

His visits home were brief and widely spaced because of the distance. He got used to doing without his family. He wasn't an orphan, nor did homesickness take hold of him; rather, he felt unattached, the freer to move whenever a new path would open for him.

Elias quit his job at the hat shop. There was no future for him in Hungary, he wrote to his parents. He heard from other aspiring young men that manual laborers were needed to work in the salt mines of France. He'd succeeded in getting a visa and a contract, and took the next train to France. After fulfilling his two-year obligation to the salt company, Elias moved to Paris, where he found work as a deliveryman for a manufacturer of children's aprons.

Eugène turned seventeen in 1929. He was now skilled and profitable to his master. His customers liked his work, so one day, emboldened, he asked for a real salary.

"You've been a good and faithful worker, Iene," Mr. Feldman replied, "but I have expenses and cannot afford to pay more. There isn't enough clientele in this town to accommodate several good tailors. I trained you well. Now you must find work on your own."

Eugène went home to visit his parents and report his newly acquired independent status. By chance he met up with Lazlo, one of his old classmates, who had been able to leave his native village to pursue his studies. He was back home visiting his family and spoke proudly about his life and his career. He was a pharmacist's assistant and made good money in Budapest, a great and beautiful place, so civilized, with paved sidewalks. "All kinds of people live there," said Lazlo, "intellectuals, artists, novelists, and politicians, mingling freely together."

PART ONE—EUGÈNE & CARMEN
CHAPTER TWO

Jews were accepted in these circles and were not afraid to speak out on any topic, Lazlo said. "We have wonderful cafés where we meet almost daily. My favorite is the Hungaria, beautiful inside and out, entirely Art Nouveau."

He noticed Eugène's blank face and explained, "Art Nouveau is a style of architecture, with flowing lines and distinctive motifs that make stones into flowers and iron into snakes."

"Oh, I see," said Eugène, not really seeing. "Thank you for explaining."

"At the Hungaria," continued his friend, "Viennese coffee and pastries are served morning to night, and not one evening passes without some interesting entertainment. We have political discussions, concerts, poetry readings, philosophical debates and the like. We shout, we clap, we drink, and we laugh. If nothing important is happening, we smoke cigars and play cards until closing time. That's the place for a smart young man like you, Iene. Come for a visit. I have a spare bed. I'll put you up as long as you wish."

Eugène still didn't know what 'Art Nouveau' looked like. He'd never drunk real coffee, just the cheaper, bitter barley that was the common fare in the impoverished villages. He didn't understand the conviviality of a card game, had never read or heard any poetry, knew nothing about politics. But he imagined the rooms with the dim lights his friend described, their red glow, the sculpted wood of the coffee tables, and overall the buzz of conversations.

Now he felt starved hearing about pastries and the never-ending excitement someone living in Budapest enjoyed. Wistfulness took hold of him. He longed to get away from his present life, yearned to join a world shinier than his own. It became his most ardent desire to learn about new things and see other places. But the trip would make a dent in his meager savings. Besides, he felt cloddish and uneducated. Would he be able to fit in?

Lazlo insisted, "Look, you've never been anywhere. The world's an apple. Take a bite! Furthermore, you're in luck, pal. My girlfriend was supposed to come to meet my parents. She's a talented actress. A real beauty! We're engaged to be married. Well, her agent called at the last minute. She couldn't miss the audition. So I have an extra train ticket in my pocket. Yours for the taking. What do you say? You can stay in my apartment; perhaps make me a suit while you're there. I'll buy the cloth and pay you good money. I've got lots of acquaintances; you'll get more work than you need."

Eugène was speechless for a moment; he looked at Lazlo. Was he serious?

"Well, what about it?" asked Lazlo impatiently. "Do you have a job, a better offer? I doubt you'll find one, especially in this hole of a place."

Eugène fast regained his wits; he knew his friend was right and accepted his offer thankfully.

Budapest was everything Lazlo said. Wonder upon wonder! A different country! The streets and shops, lit late into the evening, gave him a sharp inner vision; enlightenment shone on him. Why, he would become the tailor of the Budapest intelligentsia.

At the Hungaria, men and women wore fine, sometimes extravagant clothes, the likes of which he'd never seen before. Eugène set himself free of the past fashions to adapt his style to the current ones. He became curious and wanted to see everything. He took time to

PART ONE—EUGÈNE & CARMEN
CHAPTER TWO

walk around the city without Lazlo's guidance.

One day he found himself in front of an imposing white building from which flew a blue, white, and red flag. He recognized it immediately. Elias had sent him a postcard of the tricolors, swelling in the wind close to the Eiffel Tower. "The celebration of the French Revolution, on the fourteenth of July," Elias had written on the back of the photograph. Eugène was standing in front of the French Embassy in Budapest. A line of people waited on one side of the embassy. He walked to the back of the queue and approached the young man standing in front of him.

"May I ask what are you waiting for?" he inquired.

"I am applying for a visa," the man answered.

"To do what?"

"To allow me to study in France."

Eugène's ears buzzed; he heard his brother's voice urging him to join him in Paris. Up to now, he had been a drop of water in a wave, inconsequential, lost in the mass. The sudden impulse to leave his country became, in short, an obsession.

He entered the queue, giddy with the possibility that a move away from Hungary to another country might enrich a young man's life. His turn in the line came; he fairly flew in front of a clerk who wearily asked his name. The clerk wrote it on a document, stamped it, and said, "Student visa. Valid for two years."

Student visa, indeed! He, who had never gone beyond the sixth grade! Eugène congratulated himself heartily and rushed to send Elias a telegram alerting him of his incipient arrival. He worked hard to finish Lazlo's suit, as well as some skirts and pants for Lazlo's girlfriend, for which his friend paid most generously. Finally, he took a trip home to say goodbye to his parents.

"It's good knowing that you and Elias will be together, my son," said his father, whose sight was diminishing. And his mother, dear sweet Fanny, for whom conversation was like white bread, an unknown luxury that didn't fit in a day filled with chores, made a single request.

"Don't forget to send us postcards and photographs, my son."

Little did Eugène know he would never see either of his parents again. Fanny died quietly in her sleep, a well-earned kind of death, five long years before Hitler began implementing the terrible events leading to *Kristallnacht* and beyond.

A long journey was ahead of him. The train traveled slowly, trailing a thick scarf of smoke through the mountains, fields, and cities of Austria, Germany, and France. He never closed his eyes, wanting to absorb everything, dizzy with the motion and shapes of alternating patterns of fields revolving like magic carpets around him.

The locomotive pulled him across a bridge on the mighty Rhine into France with the ease of a seasoned long-distance runner. It stopped in Strasbourg, where many people spoke a German dialect he understood a little. Watching boarding travelers, hearing their shouting and laughing made him feel his own isolation. Suddenly, Eugène realized that the part of his life that was already so many kilometers behind was fast shrinking, its remnants receding like disintegrating ghosts. Here and now he was afloat, without anchor, on the verge of a new life, undefined and uncertain. Instinctively, he reached for his scant belongings, opened his suitcase and pulled out

PART ONE—EUGÈNE & CARMEN
CHAPTER TWO

his sewing kit, examined the tailor's chalk, the shiny thimble, a set of new needles and the heavy scissors with fine blades that cut neatly through layers of cloth without fraying it. He felt comforted. He was on a quest to refashion the world and make it fit into a shape he could hang in a closet for safekeeping at night.

Chapter Three

Eugène arrived in Paris around noon on a rainy November day in 1929, pulled Elias' address out of his pocket, and showed it to one of the taxi drivers waiting in front of the cavernous Gare du Nord train station. It was an ordinary weekday, but to his surprise, the streets were filled with people looking both reverent and subdued. Long lines of cars made for slow traffic.

His driver seemed to be going in a roundabout way. His gestures and words were probably meant as an explanation, but Eugène didn't understand what the man was trying to explain. All the same, he nodded now and then, not wanting to appear impolite to this representative of the great country of France.

Only later did he discover why so few people were at work that day. Georges Clemenceau, a beloved hero of the World War I, nicknamed "The Tiger" by his admirers, had just died. He had been a senator, a minister of the interior, and the author of *Grandeur and Misery of Victory*, an analysis of the Great War, which Clemenceau believed should have ended all subsequent ones because of its absurd brutality. Many years later Eugène saw a portrait of Clemenceau painted by the Impressionist artist Manet. It showed a man of short stature with quite ordinary features, whose looks belied the passion and the devotion he showed for justice. But what personally endeared him to this man of action was his tenaciously vocal defense of Alfred Dreyfus, the Jewish officer wrongly accused of treason by the top echelon of the French army.

At some point during that snail-like taxi ride to his brother's apartment, he spotted the silhouette of the Eiffel Tower, tall and graceful, with a women's figure, corseted in a long, lacy metal gown. She seemed to be expecting his visit, and he was eager to meet her; but Elias had sent a telegram before his departure. He had found a job for his brother and was anxious to see him. They were to go to a tailor's shop immediately upon his arrival. The tower would have to wait.

Mr. Landau, the tailor, was Polish by birth. He addressed Eugène in French, then in Yiddish. Eugène knew not a word of either language. Most Eastern European Jews spoke Yiddish, but not Hungarians. Mr. Landau was an easily irritated fellow. He threw down a stack of sleeves and their linings near a sewing machine. The task was not the kind a skilled tailor would waste his time on. Eugène was no longer an apprentice, but he was polite and did the work rapidly. Landau stood right over him and made him feel nervous and unsure of himself. He was like a turtle flipped on his back. Landau examined the work. He grabbed the sleeves away with a heavy sigh and motioned Eugène toward an ironing board. The interview was over; he had been brutally demoted. He didn't understand what he had done wrong.

Perhaps the work of tailoring was not the same in France as in Hungary. He had already noticed the unfamiliar style and cut of the clothes people wore. What the Parisians wore did not resemble his own suit, which he knew to be in the latest Budapest fashion. By comparison it appeared skimpy and abnormally shortwaisted.

PART ONE—EUGÈNE & CARMEN
CHAPTER THREE

Back on the street, along the elegant Avenue Montaigne, he saw a woman nudging her friend. She was giggling and pointing her finger at him. So be it; style, like custom, is a conjunction of time and place. The true tailor is the one who isn't afraid to change and innovate. That was the philosophy of his trade, one that has gone a long way toward the adaptability of its practitioners.

"The problem," said Landau to Elias, who came back with his brother early the next morning to see what had gone wrong, "is that your brother doesn't know how to speak a civilized language. So I can't tell him his work is ok, is fine, better than fine. But the way he does it! It's just not profitable. What I want is someone both skilled and fast, a jaguar on a machine."

Back home, in Hungary, his master used to point at the illustrated calendar pinned to the wall of the shop and say, "You see, Eugène; Rome wasn't built in one day. Look at that Coliseum there, still standing after more than two thousand years. Our customers want to wear their suits for a good long time too. You have to reassure them. When they order from us, they want something that lasts, a piece of immortality. Every stitch must be tight, yet invisible. Good work takes time."

But there was no pleasing Mr. Landau. Eugène was not a sprinter; he refused to do a shoddy job. Fortunately, the weekend arrived. Elias took him on his first ride on the Métro to meet friends and introduce his brother to the members of the Hungarian club where new and old immigrants mingled.

The happiness he felt at being able to communicate again was indescribable. His lack of French had turned him into a mute, shut out from the world of feelings and ideas. He had never been so conscious of his voice, of the joy he derived from hearing it. The sounds growing in his throat and in his mouth rolled on his tongue. They vibrated simultaneously through his head, made their way deep inside his viscera, drumming there the certainty of his presence in the world.

His family would later say he was a big talker who would die if he had to be quiet even for only one day. This was true. He did not dispute it. More than once in his life, Eugène would have to leave everything he owned, everyone with whom he carried a meaningful relationship, his parents, his wife, and his children. Yet no one would ever be able to rob him of his voice. It was a reliable companion and would help save him from all kinds of dangers. He used it later in the worst of circumstances, during his long captivity, as a last resort when diffusing the anger of a menacing guard, and for the best when striking a halting conversation with a fellow prisoner whose mother tongue was different from his. "Yes," he'd say, "I owe my life to two things: my needle and my voice, both the lightest and most useful of tools to carry."

An immigrant's club is a cocoon, encapsulating sense of self and community in the midst of the wider world of native speakers, who already possess linguistic proficiency. Elias knew and talked to everyone. He introduced Eugène, "My kid brother, from the old country. A fine tailor who is eager to work." A short man with a big smile on his face came toward Eugène and shook his hand. He had long teeth and a horsey face. "Michel Szego," he said, with a strong Hungarian accent, "*Moi, je fais des bijoux.*" He flashed a big gold ring in Eugène's face while tapping his chest with pride. "I design jewelry,"

PART ONE—EUGÈNE & CARMEN
CHAPTER THREE

he repeated in Hungarian. Michel Szego was a countryman two years older than himself, a craftsman and a jeweler, a bit of a braggart who made a good living selling his creations to select jewelry shops. They became and remained friends until Szego died at a ripe old age.

Szego lost no time in introducing Eugène to a Hungarian tailor of his acquaintance who had a large clientele and needed additional staff. Erwin Farkas had several employees, each with special strengths and skills, but not any one capable of manufacturing an entire garment. He'd remedied that by instituting a kind of assembly line that allowed him to capitalize on the ability of each and every employee. Eugène was delighted to demonstrate the kind of work he could do. Farkas was impressed; he handed Eugène a stack of trade fashion magazines said, "Copy the words, learn the terms, and look at the patterns. Come back in two days. Here's some money. Get yourself some food and don't waste time." Thus *col, manche, taille, ourlet, biais,* and *epaulettes* became Eugène's first acquisitions in French vocabulary.

A year later, Elias left Paris with his wife, mother-in-law, and infant daughter. He opened a millinery in the city of Clermont-Ferrand in the Auvergne, 346 kilometers south of Paris. With Elias gone, Eugène was now completely on his own. Fortunately he had his good friend—"Little Szego," as everyone called him—around the same age as he, without a family of his own. The two men bonded, treating each other like lifelong relatives. Without Szego, he would never have found as good a boss as Mr. Farkas. However, after several months learning the Paris trade Eugène decided to move on from the status of employee to that of independent tailor. He was ready to start a business of his own. There were enormous obstacles; he had neither capital to expand, nor money to lease a shop or buy the bolts of cloth he would show to future clientele.

"You're wrong, *mon ami*, I thought about it. It can be done," said Szego. "What are friends for? I will be your creditor. You'll repay me a little at a time. It's a good deal for both of us."

A loan was something Eugène had never thought of asking from anyone. With the money Szego offered, he soon found a two-room apartment in the fourth arrondissement of Paris, near the rue des Rosiers, then and now the main artery through the predominantly Jewish neighborhood. He also bought a secondhand sewing machine in order to work at home. Immediately after, he made the rounds of the successful tailoring establishments and workshops of his new neighborhood. Alterations were needed everywhere. He got plenty of work, which he always finished and returned well ahead of deadlines. He was fast developing a good reputation, and after two years had enough savings to repay Szego and launch a new venture. Henceforth, he would be working under his own name, producing custom-made suits for his own clientele.

Of course, his first patron was Szego. He had ordered two summer suits at once. Eugène had selected the fabrics, blue and black cloth with discrete pinstripes that created a *trompe l'oeil* effect, lengthening his short friend's silhouette. Szego wore each suit in turn for the more formal parties held at the Hungarian club.

Most people describe themselves as too tall, too fat, or too skinny. It's up to their tailor to fulfill their desire for perfection. Several of his Hungarian club's countrymen came to Eugène with special requests. He promised to do his best, took their measurements and

PART ONE—EUGÈNE & CARMEN
CHAPTER THREE

recommended styles. Their steady satisfaction meant more customers. Everything happened by word of mouth, and little by little he even found genuine French-born patrons.

One of them worked at City Hall and helped him get a work permit. He was entering a new world and had cards printed with the words:

EUGÈNE TAILLEUR
18 rue des Tournelles
Paris IVème
Métro ◊ Bastille

Life was good. He was twenty years old and his own boss. He loved France and the French, and his language skills improved greatly. Whenever he found time, he read voraciously, especially the newspapers, those of the left as well as those of the right, enlightening himself about the political currents that were wrenching French society and the rest of Europe. He was able to carry conversations on multiple topics and gained enough assurance to exchange opinions with his customers. He often needed the help of a dictionary, and he wrote a personal lexicon with words he studied until he learned the meaning of each. Later, he began reading a novel by Jack London in a French translation. He identified with the struggle of London's working-class heroes and measured his own hard-earned success to theirs. He also revered Victor Hugo and his creation, Jean Valjean, the hero of *Les Misérables*, condemned to hard labor for stealing a loaf of bread. Reborn, after serving time, as Monsieur Madeleine, Valjean becomes a legitimate bourgeois doing good deeds. The orphan he adopts becomes the love of his life; later on, he joins the young leaders who are fighting for democracy, civil rights, and reforms. The abject poverty of the revolutionaries, their passion and fervor, their cold-eyed dissection of the politics of those times; all of that fascinated Eugène. He saw himself on the barricades. But then, he wondered, were there ever times without ills, without wars?

Chapter Four

Eugène had been lucky enough to obtain a work permit when he did, though full citizenship was out of the question. The prevalent xenophobia in France, and the political tensions between the Right and the Left, created a climate in which noncitizens like Eugène became an easy target. Their status was precarious. By the mid-thirties, the ultra-Right government was deporting former guest workers as well as refugees.

The Nationalists made no bones about it. They feared and disliked foreign people and foreign cultures. Their opponents, supporters of the Left, the Liberals, Socialists, and Communists, claimed they were joining the fight for universal rights and against fascism. However, when firm language and action to fight discrimination and racism were called for, the Left parties caved in. They did not protest against those who banned the popular American artist Josephine Baker from performing her electrifying dances, deemed immoral by many of them. Yet Baker demonstrated what she stood for during the war when she joined the French Resistance. Her valiant actions made her a hero and, by contrast, shamed her detractors, Nationalist or otherwise, many of whom became collaborators.

Unfortunately for Eugène and his Jewish friends, most of them recent arrivals from Central and Eastern Europe, the greatest financial scandal of the pre-war years involved a shadowy Ukrainian Jewish immigrant who amassed enormous wealth in an amazingly short time. He was cool, smooth, and handsome, wore elegant cream-colored suits and impeccably pressed shirts. Anyone looking at him in the photographs that appeared in the press would have believed him to be a movie star, rather than the professional crook he turned out to be.

However, the elegantly clad Alexandre Stavisky's fortune was tainted; the money came from laundering operations involving several members of the French government. To everyone's surprise, Stavisky committed suicide just before his impending arrest. The newspapers suggested that the police had conveniently engineered his death. Stavisky knew too much; his revelations could have implicated many of his government accomplices. Public indignation and unrest came to a boiling point when the lifeless body of the judge in charge of the investigation was found. His death, reported to have occurred under violent conditions, remained unexplained. People grew angry and took to the streets. Serious confrontations ensued. A vociferous protest from supporters of the Right was followed by an equally loud counter-protest of the Left, who denounced the machinations of the leaders of the country.

Eugène and his friends belonged to the latter faction. As immigrants and as Jews they felt targeted. Because of that, they eagerly joined the large parade making its way to the Bastille. "Neither racist fascists, nor profiteers will prevail," resounded their rallying cry.

One thousand, four hundred thirty-five people were wounded during the demonstration. Fifteen others died in the melee that involved the rival factions and the police. Eugène was lucky to go home, hoarse from

PART ONE—EUGÈNE & CARMEN
CHAPTER FOUR

screaming, and with a black eye received in the heat of things. Almost weekly for the next two years, the Right, fueled by *Action Française*, a racist, openly anti-Semitic rag, marched from the wealthy district of the Champs Élysées to the ultra-Nationalist Etoile. The Left, honoring its roots, regrouped at the Populist Père Lachaise cemetery where the Communards of the previous century staged their last stand and withstood the bullets of a vengeful reactionary government.

Despite the unrest in France and in Europe, Eugène and his friends enjoyed some lighthearted moments. Sports of all types attracted their interest, none more than the Tour de France. In 1930, they faithfully and enthusiastically followed the trajectory of the 24th Tour de France on their radios. That year the organizers added a new element. Instead of celebrating only one winner among the participants, they created an innovative contest between five national teams, each running with eight teammates. Five countries participated: Belgium, Italy, Spain, Germany, and France, each sending their best legs to the fearlessly contested first place. It was a war on wheels won by André Leducq. France proudly celebrated with fireworks and dancing in the streets.

The whole Hungarian club flocked en masse to each of the numerous soccer games held in the Colombes Stadium in the spring of 1931. Eugène and Szego departed early for fear their assigned seats might be given away. France and Germany were facing one another, and a huge crowd of 40,000 shouted endlessly for the two rivals. Like everyone else in the stadium, Eugène and Szego cheered until their throats were hoarse, and their heads dizzy.

Soccer is not the kind of sport that demands that the players be a certain height or weight. This is what makes it a democratic game. What does matter is that the player displays speed, passion, and intelligence. The soccer players, young, wiry fellows of average height, who came from ordinary and often modest family backgrounds, had learned to outrun life and find their own place in the sun. *L'Équipe*, the national sport newspaper, related that most of them had trained on vacant lots behind buildings and in the streets, as Eugène had done in his youth.

The spectators found the cunning, the speed, and the skill of these sportsmen unusual. They were awesome, astonishing athletes. Energized by their passion, the crowd understood their fervor, felt their sweat, ran with their legs, and kicked the ball to the winning goal. Great soccer prevailed, and in the end their countrymen, deemed favorites by the sportscasters, won. Eugène and Szego returned home satisfied. For a few days all of France, whether from the Right or the Left, united, inebriated by the flush of victory. It was as if a flow of love had transformed the nation into one big, gregarious family.

Chapter Five

Eugène and Szego often double dated. They went out with several girls from the Hungarian club, though nothing serious ensued for either one of them. Altogether this was a season of easy camaraderie that suited the tailor and the jeweler while steady work kept them busy.

One day Szego took Eugène to Goldenberg's, a deli he frequented ever after. They needed food for a picnic. They were going to the Bois de Vincennes, a lovely wooded enclave on the easternmost side of Paris, to attend a rally organized by the Socialist party.

"Clara, meet my friend Eugène," said Szego to the young woman behind the counter.

They shook hands. Clara was a red head with fiery blue eyes and a firm handshake.

"Pretty and slender, but she limps. Still a catch!" Szego informed him as they left. "She practically runs the deli by herself. She is a true workhorse. Her brother—he plays the violin—shows no interest in the store. He gets hives just smelling pickles."

But Eugène wasn't interested. He liked the freedom and the uncomplicated home he was making for himself. Women meant responsibility, children, obligations, and expenses so far as he could see when he observed his married friends.

"Why don't you take her out yourself?" he asked Szego.

"I'm too short," he sighed. "Even with her limp, she towers over me."

Eugène returned to Goldenberg's alone and soon made it a weekly errand. Inevitably, he and Clara became friends. She clearly liked him and wasn't shy about letting it be known. Before long, she asked him if he'd like to go to the movies with her.

He had never had a relationship with a woman, not even in Budapest where he'd met several stylish ladies at Lazlo's house. He felt intimidated by these witty, smartly dressed Parisian girls and could not imagine any of them showing any interest in him.

He felt more at ease with Clara and accepted her invitation, though not without some trepidation. Night had just arrived; they found each other at the Gaumont movie theater. Clara ran toward him with a slight limp and kissed him on the cheek. He dared not say anything, and hardly had time to recover his wits when she let out a sharp whistle.

"My, my, you look like a real movie star!" she said admiringly.

Of course, he was overdressed and uncomfortable. He had to be the only man in the movie theater wearing a good suit.

That night, he fell in love with Marlene Dietrich. She had the starring role in *The Blue Angel*. Her mixture of ferocity and loveliness magnetized him. How could one avoid falling in love with such a woman? He was so absorbed in his contemplation of Dietrich that he hardly noticed that Clara was holding his hand. Later, they walked in the dark streets, their arms around each other's waist. He played his part as a gallant and found that he enjoyed it.

PART ONE—EUGÈNE & CARMEN
CHAPTER FIVE

A week later, Clara invited him for supper at her parents' home where he unwittingly caused quite a stir. He was lanky and svelte in those days, darkly handsome with his thick, curly, black hair. He knew women found him good looking. He stared in his mirror and agreed with them. It was a reassuring feeling, though he tried not to dwell on his appearance.

Clara's father, however, did not seem so impressed. He spoke sharply to his daughter in a fast Yiddish he didn't understand. Clara's mother began crying; Eugène thought about leaving, but Clara was determined. "Hand me your identity card," she said. Her father scrutinized it. After a while he nodded, shrugged his shoulders, and without looking at Eugène threw the card back on the table.

This incident changed Eugène's mind. His role as the gallant was suddenly less appealing. Still, he liked Clara's blue eyes, her turned-up button nose, and her bright copper hair. Her limp didn't bother him in the least. Indeed, it was hardly noticeable. Clever, funny, loving, and hard working, she was indeed a catch.

One thrilling night they made love at his place. It was a revelation, a grand *Quatorze Juillet* celebration. But he questioned himself: what if Clara had gotten pregnant? Why should he rush to establish a family? He was only twenty-two years old. His work already kept him busier than he wanted to be. Furthermore, he was not inclined to trade his sewing machine to sell gefilte fish and pickles behind the counter as Clara suggested. He would be bored serving customers for hours, smiling at each in turn, asking how he could help them, and thanking them for their purchases. His trade was an artistic endeavor; selling meat and sandwiches was mere bartering. And, finally, he liked being his own boss, working at his own pace, while listening to the radio.

That talking box had become his school and his university. Everything he heard on his radio intrigued him. He listened attentively to the politicians airing their views. He was part of their debates, spoke out loud, applauded or refuted their comments. And then came the popular singers, philosophers of a kind, and sportscasters with their glib reporting of various sports, boxing matches, and bicycle races.

He had to be honest with Clara. He explained as well as he could that he was not ready for married life. She cried, begged him to reconsider, and then changed the subject. Why, she would buy him a brand-new, expensive radio to replace his old one.

"The static and buzzing that box emits," she declared. There was some truth to that, but it did not bother him. He knew how to correct that nuisance. She finally gave up, brokenhearted. He gave his business to the other Goldenberg's delicatessen, run by a cousin of Clara's father.

Chapter Six

Eugène still met his brother Elias from time to time, especially when Elias had business in Paris. Elias would spend the day buying merchandise he needed for his shop in Clermont-Ferrand. He always stayed overnight in a hotel in the fourth arrondissement near the Bastille and left in the morning to go back home to his family.

The brothers met in the evening for dinner to talk about the latest news from Hungary. Their parents were managing to put some food on their table with the produce they grew, but Samuel's sight was worse, and Fanny suffered from arthritis in her hands. They needed financial help to see doctors and cover sundry expenditures. The two brothers sent as much money as they could spare to help Samuel and Fanny survive.

Elias was an inveterate talker; he liked to embellish things. He was the proud father of a seven-year-old daughter. "Eveline is very smart," he gloated. "She is already a grade ahead of her class. She studies English and can already speak like an American."

"Really!" Eugène teased him. "You're raising a little genius. Are you sure you are the father?"

Eugène could have taken the metro that particular evening he'd set aside to see Elias. Instead, he decided to jog to the hotel. It was cold, though winter had not yet arrived, but he needed some exercise after a long day of bending over the sewing machine. The streets were filled with people buying their supper baguettes and hurrying home. Others congregated in cafés. Through the windows he could see the sullied, smoky air within, moving like an undulating veil.

It was reassuring to be part of a crowd, to feel alone yet mingling with others. Perhaps it was romantic on his part to assume that any individual who crossed his path was the satisfied member of a contented society. He knew better, of course. He had eyes and ears, but he was also trustful and enthusiastic, and had not yet experienced the tragedy of war that would befall Europe and catch him in its net.

It was good to run through the crowded, narrow streets, just to feel himself running. He was looking forward to dinner with his brother, and, upon reaching rue Elzévir, nearly bumped into a young woman waiting outside.

"So sorry," he said. "My apologies, Mademoiselle."

"No harm. Do you live here?" the young woman asked in halting French.

"No, I don't live here. My brother does. He rents a room on the first floor, but I never go up there. We have an agreement. He leaves the window open, and I whistle for him to come down. Are you locked out?"

She smiled hesitantly. He surmised she did not quite understand what he was saying.

"Watch," he said. He took a few steps back and whistled loudly. Elias appeared at the window and shouted back, "Here I come!" Seconds later the door opened, and out came his brother.

"Well, Miss, your waiting is over," said Eugène holding the heavy door for her.

PART ONE—EUGÈNE & CARMEN
CHAPTER SIX

"Thank you," she replied, bringing her hands to her mouth, blowing warmth into them. She was shivering without gloves or hat, attempting to stretch a thin cotton jacket over her body, which offered little protection against a cool September night with a rising wind.

Elias and Eugène embraced. "Your new friend?" Elias asked, pointing to the young woman.

"No, we literally bumped into each other," said Eugène with a warm smile. "But you, Elias, have just saved that young lady. She forgot her key to the door and has been waiting in the cold for someone to come to her rescue."

Elias had a friendly quality or a fault, depending on whether the person getting his attention accepted him or not. He could never resist talking to any one in reach, whether acquaintance or stranger.

"Wait, young lady," he said, "You look like you're freezing! Tell you what, come with us and get a bite to eat. It will warm you up. Then we'll walk you back here and escort you in."

She didn't answer, just kept looking at Elias. He shrugged.

"Maybe she's a deaf mute," he murmured. But he did not give up and turned toward her, rapidly miming someone eating a meal. He smacked his lip once or twice, looking quite grotesque in Eugène's opinion. To his surprise, the young woman smiled, nodded her head up and down, and said, "yes, yes" eagerly. She must have been very hungry to go with perfect strangers. Elias chattered all the way to the restaurant, obtaining a "yes" or a "no" from time to time, which encouraged him to go on with his soliloquies. They finally arrived at the restaurant and were seated at a table for three.

Eugène didn't dare look directly at the impromptu guest, though he noticed her great head of blond curls. He was fascinated; they reminded him of the wheat fields of Tyukod on a summer day.

Elias ordered three *plats du jour* and a bottle of wine.

"Well, young lady, you can tell us everything about yourself. Where are you from? What's your name? What sort of work do you do?"

"Elias," Eugène whispered, "don't be rude, you'll scare her! I don't think she understands what you're talking about."

"What? My French isn't good enough for her? Perhaps I'm speaking too fast. It's a bad habit of mine, but . . ." Elias tapped his head, suddenly inspired.

"Do you speak Hungarian, perhaps Polish, maybe German?"

"Ja, ja, German," she nodded happily, visibly relieved.

Both Elias and Eugène had learned a little German during their schooling in Tyukod, not by choice but because they had to, as a sort of tribute Hungarian citizens paid to the former and larger Austrian empire of which not too long ago they had still been a part.

"My name is Carmen, Carmen Tieme. I was born in Strasbourg and raised in Nuremberg where my family settled. I am nineteen years old and have just arrived in Paris." The words were now tumbling out of her mouth.

"Carmen, eh?" Elias laughed. "What kind of German name is that?"

"My father likes operas. Carmen is his favorite."

"Ah, so your parents like classical music. Are they here with you?"

"No, I'm alone. I came by myself. To study," Carmen blushed. "I want to be a psychologist, but first I need to find work. I hope really soon."

"You came without money?"

"No, I have a little. My room's paid for a month."

PART ONE—EUGÈNE & CARMEN
CHAPTER SIX

"Your parents should have given you more! This is Paris. Without money, you'll wind up living under a bridge, and the weather is not getting any warmer."

"I had not much time to plan. It's my mother, you know, she is cruel. She took me out of school, and she made me her maid. I decided to leave. I ran away from home with the little money I saved. I couldn't take it anymore. Anyway, Nuremberg is a grim place nowadays. You never know when thugs will start pushing people around. I want to be free from that, to have a different life here in Paris."

She spoke with a mixture of despair and defiance. Her seagreen eyes mirrored the depth of her emotions and turned darker as she went on.

"I understand. Are you Jewish?" asked Elias.

She hesitated. "What difference does it make to you?"

"None. Excuse him for being so direct," said Eugène.

The brothers looked at each other; they too had left parents and homeland behind and struggled to find work and learn a new language. They felt sorry for Carmen. She seemed so alone, so young, nearly a child.

"I want to work," she said, "but people keep asking for papers. I have only a copy of my birth certificate."

"The border police let you in with just a birth certificate?"

"I followed a family when the train stopped. I acted as if I were part of their group. It wasn't difficult. And if you need to know, I'm not hiding it. Yes, I am Jewish."

The more she spoke, the more Eugène's heart went out to her. She appeared naïve in contrast to his mature twenty-plus years, yet he perceived a boundless strength in her and admired her without restraint.

He was falling in love: it was a *coup de foudre*, a thunderbolt, as the French say, a brand-new experience, one he embraced. He dwelt in the moment in a state of elation. He felt it was his duty to help her. He told her Elias and he would be her friends. Everything would turn out all right.

He turned to his elder brother and asked, "What can we do, what should we do?"

His brother was a man who had faced many dramatic and dangerous situations in his wandering life. He had also learned to react quickly.

"Try to get her some papers, I guess. Easier, if you married her," he suggested with a wink. He continued chuckling, "I'm already married, or else I would have been happy to ask her to be my bride because I'm a good guy, just to help, of course. But let's be serious. What about that client of yours, you know, the one who helped you gain your work permit? Bet he could do something."

"No marriage," Carmen interjected with fiery cheeks. "I am young and strong. I'll clean houses if I have to."

Eugène, too, felt himself reddening. Elias, that devil, had sensed his sudden interest in Carmen. Trying to extricate himself from having to explain everything, he hastened to reply, "Oh yes, Monsieur Chatelet! That's a thought. I'll go see him next week."

They finished their meal. Elias had Eugène write a few words to their parents on a postcard he was sending them. He was leaving Paris the next day and invited Eugène to come visit him and his family in Clermont-Ferrand. The brothers embraced, then Elias and Carmen walked back to rue Elzévir.

Eugène went home feeling supremely happy, so light he could have flown up, up, up, and danced upon a rooftop like a Chagall character smiling at his blue cow. Carmen had agreed to meet him again.

Chapter Seven

The year was 1886; Zurich was a bustling community where Jews had only recently been readmitted. These new citizens were proving themselves an enterprising lot, enthusiastically participating in the legal and medical professions and practicing time-honored trades, such as designing and smelting jewels, tailoring, and brewing. They invested in all kinds of new commerce in this modern, mercantile city. Sol Tieme, Carmen's father, a well-educated, ambitious young man, was making his way to the synagogue. It was Rosh Hashanah.

Be they rich, middle class, or poor, the Jewish citizens of Zurich reserved their best clothes for the High Holy days. They came early to get a good seat from which to observe new arrivals to the great hall of the synagogue where the service took place. The married ladies discreetly observed each other's dress, assessing the refinement of delicate lace and embroidery, the luster of pearls on the padded bosom of the well-to-do members of the community. They whispered remarks having to do with good taste, or lack of. Comparisons, denigrations, admiration, and excitement swelled to a buzz, filling the pews of the temple, until the rabbi and the cantor made their appearance on the podium. Hushed laughter persisted for a minute or so, then subsided.

A moment later Berta Weiss walked in with her family, unwittingly smiting young Sol Tieme with a lazy gaze that went straight to his heart. There and then, he decided he wanted her to be his bride. He was sure he could make it happen—his plans always developed as he wished. He even knew where they would marry: in London, a city he had seen only on postcards and travel brochures, which his imagination endowed as the true residence of civilization and grace.

Berta's sister, a gawky girl named Erna, as effaced as Berta was effervescent, followed their stolid mother. The ceremony began as the Weiss family came in.

"On the edge of late, I'd say," murmured one woman to another. "Poor Mrs. Weiss, look at her red cheeks! You know she's so embarrassed."

"Berta's fault," murmured one of the girl's classmates in Sol's hearing. "She always arrives after the morning bell. Of course if anyone else behaved as she does, teacher would send her to the principal."

Berta's father, a respected and dutiful man, was the acting president of the congregation and the owner of the Muzlay Beer Brewery. As such, Mrs. Weiss reminded her daughters, "Our family has responsibilities that befit us to behave respectfully." Berta liked to stay up late into the night, and then sleep late into the morning, despite remonstrations from her mother, who was known to be as punctual as the ringing of the city tower bell.

Sol began questioning himself. Was it possible for him to enter the circles of society in which Berta revolved? The answer was not long in coming. He decided to quit his job and apply for a clerk's position in the accounting department of the Muzlay Beer Brewery. Indeed, he

PART ONE—EUGÈNE & CARMEN
CHAPTER SEVEN

was hired in early January, just in time to join the rest of the employees at the annual party given by Mr. Weiss and his family. This, he thought, was a good omen, the kind of opportunity he'd hoped for.

Mr. Weiss addressed his guests and had good news: Muzlay Beer was eclipsing rival brands. The brew production must be doubled and new personnel hired. He had already engaged some new people and was about to introduce them to the assembly and to his family.

Sol Tieme moved to the end of the reception line. He meant to be last to approach the boss and leave him with a favorable impression. However, he was shaking hands with the female members of the family when the orchestra began to play a waltz. He was now standing before Berta. What was more natural than inviting her for a dance? The young lady responded with a nod and a smile.

A charming couple they made. She was wearing a green taffeta dress, swishing with each turn of the waltz. She felt the looks of others all around, as she listened to her impeccably dressed chevalier. He spoke passionately about travel, music, and literature. The young lady approved—she too wanted adventure and travel to foreign countries—and Sol promised both. A few months of courtship later, they were engaged. They married in London, lived in Strasbourg for a few years, and then eventually settled in Nuremberg, Germany, with their three children: Maurice, Carmen, and Sonia.

Chapter Eight

Eugène delivered the suit Monsieur Chatelet had ordered, but had not heard from his client since. He could only hope he was pleased with the work. He did not have time to make a proper appointment and gambled that Monsieur Chatelet would see him without one. It was his desire to act as quickly as possible on Carmen's behalf. Early the next day, he went to City Hall to speak to Chatelet. The clerk at the front desk said that Monsieur was busy. "Wait for him if you like, but he won't be available for another hour at the very least," the clerk said.

To pass time, Eugène bought a newspaper and sat down to read it in a café. For months, the headlines on the front page had shouted frightening news. On 30 January 1933, Hitler was appointed Chancellor of the Reich. In February, Hitler's National Socialist German Workers Party became the largest party in the Reichstag. Prior to that, President Hindenburg had signed an emergency decree supressing Germans' civil liberties. This, he said, was an action taken to protect the state from its enemies. By that time, Hitler's enemies were the Communists. Then someone set fire to the Reichstag. A young man was arrested; he was accused of being a communist sympathizer. The Nazis took this opportunity to arrest the leaders of Germany's Communist Party and put them on trial for treason. Eugène was shocked.

His throat went dry. "Let's lay our cards upon the table," he grimly thought. "Germany is in the hands of Hitler. What terrible events are we in for?" he wondered.

What would this mean for Carmen? She was a German citizen, a foreigner in France without valid papers. The police might apprehend her at any moment. She would probably be interned in a French detention camp or sent back to Germany. And then she would be at the mercy of this Hitler, a man who made his intentions to get rid of the Jews explicit in *Mein Kampf*.

Before that, Eugène's thinking had been, "Hitler, so what? Just another anti-Semite. Let him rant." Only now this anti-Semite had just become the absolute leader of a country whose dissenters were rapidly being eliminated.

In some inevitable way, Eugène believed he had been appointed Carmen's personal savior. He didn't know how people fell in love. He guessed that for most, it was a slow, incremental process, complete with dates and introductions to friends and family, all leading to the planning of a ceremony. For him, his almost immediate attraction to Carmen was a rare happenstance, enhanced by a genuine desire to help her.

He returned to City Hall and waited for Monsieur Chatelet another hour despite his growing impatience. Chatelet eventually appeared with a smile.

"Sorry to have made you wait so long, Monsieur Eugène, a pleasure to see you. Now to speak about some pleasant things, I've had many compliments on the suit you made. I have taken the liberty to recommend you to family and friends. You should be getting some new customers soon. But what brings you here today? What can I do for you?"

PART ONE—EUGÈNE & CARMEN
CHAPTER EIGHT

Eugène didn't waste time going into the specifics of his story. Boldly, he explained that he had met the woman he wanted to marry. She was not a French citizen. Would she be allowed to obtain a working permit and the resident status he himself enjoyed?

"First, that depends on her nationality," stated Monsieur Chatelet.

"She is German, born in Strasbourg," Eugène answered.

"Well," said Monsieur Chatelet, "we have many requests for asylum from German refugees. They have good reasons to worry. Germany is rejecting and murdering many of its citizens. That little man with the mustache, Herr Hitler, has ascended a throne of no dissent. How far will he go? Poor Europe that hasn't even recovered from the last war!"

"I agree with you, Monsieur Chatelet, we are living on the edge of a volcano. Can you do anything to help us?"

"Well, Monsieur Eugène, I can only give you some advice. French law specifies that when a woman marries, she acquires her husband's nationality. Henceforth she will be recognized as a Hungarian citizen. Get married as soon as possible. She'll benefit from whichever privileges you have acquired. Go to your city hall district. They'll answer your questions and help you fill out the forms you must submit. Good luck. Don't hesitate to call on me if there are any problems."

They shook hands.

"One more favor, Monsieur Chatelet. Would you do us the honor of being a witness at the wedding?" asked Eugène.

"With pleasure. After all, I have the perfect suit, don't I?"

Walking back to his apartment, Eugène began to question himself. He had not apprised Carmen of his intentions. His reasonable side echoed in his ears and argued that he might wake up from his infatuation. After all, he had just met Carmen and didn't know her well enough. Might he be sorry to tie himself to her?

But no, protested his emotional side, you really love Carmen.

He would announce his intentions to Carmen and persuade her. He could not live without her. He positively would marry her, or else he'd lose her.

He returned to his apartment and worked until it was almost time for their rendezvous. He washed, shaved his face carefully, and splashed cologne on his throat. The reflection in the mirror approved and smiled back. Good sign, he thought.

Carmen was already waiting at the restaurant under the arcades of Place des Vosges where they had agreed to meet. The place was buzzing with people, which seemed strange for a weekday. But when bad news impacts a nation, people will likely congregate with friends.

The tailor in him made a quick observation. Carmen was wearing a simple flowered dress with long sleeves and, over it, a well-cut jacket made from cotton and fine merino wool. The simple elegance of her outfit spoke volumes about his lady's taste and elegance. How could he have doubted? He loved her more than ever.

He kissed her boldly on each cheek, in friendly greeting as the French do. They sat down in a protected area of the terrace and ordered lunch. They drank to each other's health and had some small talk about their surroundings. He knew a little about the history of Place des Vosges. It had been built for Henri de Navarre, fourth of the name, a Protestant who accepted conversion on the advice of Michel de Montaigne, the famous author of *The Essays*.

PART ONE—EUGÈNE & CARMEN
CHAPTER EIGHT

"Eh bien!" said Henri, who was a bon vivant and soon to be king, "Paris is well worth a mass." Thereafter, the pragmatic king ordered that, once per week, each family in the kingdom would be provided with a chicken for their pot.

"I hope I am not boring you. Maybe we should talk about other things."

"Oh, no," responded Carmen, "I love history. Who is the king on the horse in the center of the garden?"

"Louis the Thirteenth, the father of the Sun King, Louis the Fourteenth."

He told Carmen that the great Victor Hugo, who wrote *Les Misérables,* lived in an apartment situated right there in the Place des Vosges.

"Can we return to Victor Hugo some other time? I have important things to tell you," said Carmen.

"Go ahead," Eugène said. "I'm sorry, sometimes I run away with my mouth and my new learning."

Carmen admitted that she had not totally broken with her family. She had written her father the very day of her arrival in Paris to give him her address. She couldn't leave the Papa she adored without news. He had already written back; he was so relieved to know she was safe and well.

"He sent me money—as much as he could under the circumstances. But the real news is that my parents have decided to leave Germany as soon as they can wrap up their affairs. Father says that my mother cries every day. I know how she feels. It's hard to leave the country you always thought of as your home, and hard to leave everything you have established there."

"I thought you left because of your mother," Eugène said.

"May I have some water?" she asked.

He poured her a glass of water and handed it to her. She gulped it down and held her glass up for more before answering.

"Yes, that was what hurried me out of my home, but I also left because I was scared about what was happening in Nuremberg. There were frightening incidents; people beaten while the police looked the other way. My twelve-year-old sister was no longer comfortable at school. Her own teachers were harassing her. Of course, father was alarmed, but like most of his friends and acquaintances, he thought these troubles would go away."

The waiter brought a steaming hot soup and a basket of freshly cut bread. Carmen tried to continue speaking but then suddenly began sobbing without restraint. Eugène took her hand and held it until she stopped shaking.

"Papa now realizes that the situation is very bad. He says that soon Jews in Germany will not be allowed to live at all. He's been trying to convince his brothers and friends to pack their bags and run while they can. But they say he exaggerates. I'm so afraid for everybody there, for my Aunt Erna and all of the Jewish kids I grew up with."

"Your father is a smart man, Carmen. You won't have to worry about your mother and father. I'll help them as much as I can if they come to join us in France. Let's forget this misery for just one moment. I too have something important to tell you."

"Here," he said, handing her his handkerchief.

PART ONE—EUGÈNE & CARMEN
CHAPTER EIGHT

He released her hand. He wanted her to feel free before he proposed.

"Carmen, I am really fond of you. What I mean to say is, I've loved you since the first day we met, since the very moment I saw you blowing on your fingers to keep them warm. Here it is: I want to spend the rest of my life with you. I know this may not be the right time to ask you to make such an important decision, but then again, it is the right time. Things are happening so fast! We need one another."

She didn't reply immediately. He hadn't expected her to laugh, or cry, or perhaps even to kiss him right away. At long last she gave him a smile, and for the moment he felt warmed and satisfied. He spied a monarch butterfly fluttering nearby. The gardens of Place des Vosges were filled with fragrant autumnal flowers. Mothers were chatting with other mothers. Children's noise and laughter were brightening the afternoon. Everything was still as it should be on a peaceful and ordinary day.

"So you want to marry me?" Carmen said after a while. "Do you always do what your brother tells you to do?"

Eugène defended him. "Elias gives very good advice most of the time. Of course he talks too much, but at times, he is truly clairvoyant. He could see that, for me, our chance meeting meant love. I take the credit for feeling the way I do."

Carmen admitted to be overwhelmed by his declaration of love. Didn't he think they should get to know each other better?

"Of course, I'm all for that," Eugène emphasized.

She smiled again but didn't say yes. She had not yet said no either, and that led him to believe that she took some interest in him.

The waiter brought their dessert, and they savored it silently.

"Would you like to come see my apartment? We could talk," he suggested.

She agreed to come. He made some coffee and showed Carmen around. His two rooms were small and crowded with bolts of cloth. On the walls, he had hung fashion pictures cut out of trade magazines. She looked; she nodded. She did not seem impressed.

They sat on tabourets at a table for two in his equally small kitchen, and there he began relating his conversation with Monsieur Chatelet.

"Your parents are preparing to escape an unbearable situation, and you should be trying to make yours here less dangerous. Seriously, you could be deported back to Germany as an enemy alien, or have to flee somewhere else where conditions are even more difficult than here. Remember, you have no valid identity papers. You're illegal. Marry me now for safety's sake, if not for love."

"Yours is a very generous offer," she replied. "I appreciate it, and I am flattered, but I must think about it."

For the second time she had not said no, and though he wanted to, he refrained from asking her if she felt any affection for him.

It was getting late. He stood up to accompany her back to her rented room. He was surprised when she asked if she could spend the night.

"Remember, I haven't said yes yet," she insisted. "But I don't want to mislead you. I'm asking because I am scared in the dark in my hotel room. I wake up from bad dreams; I fight falling asleep the rest of the night. Yesterday was awful. No sooner had I closed my eyes, than I felt a man's hands pinning me down to the floor. The pressure on my shoulders was so real. I struggled, but I couldn't scream loudly enough. When I finally woke, I felt boneless, so weak I could hardly move."

He opened his arms to Carmen and held her tight.

PART ONE—EUGÈNE & CARMEN
CHAPTER EIGHT

"You can stay with me as long as you wish," he told her.

He put fresh sheets on his bed and prepared another sleeping place for himself on the cutting table where he often napped during the day. Carmen fell asleep in his bed immediately. He watched her for a long time. She seemed tranquil and relaxed. He knew she would become his bride and tried to imagine what life would be like with her at his side.

He left the apartment early the next day to get croissants, and on a whim bought a bouquet of daisies. By the time the coffee was brewing, Carmen woke up, yawned, and stretched herself like a cat. She greeted him with a large smile. They had breakfast at the small table in the cozy kitchen.

"The smell of good coffee in the morning is a greeting for the entire day," she declared. "And these flowers smell so fresh! After my papa, you are the first man to give me flowers."

She buried her nose in the bouquet, then grabbed a croissant and sank her pretty teeth into the buttery flakes.

"Delicious. Better than those you buy in Nuremberg. Now listen, I think you will like what I am going to tell you. I am ready to answer your question."

"What question?" Eugène teased, knowing perfectly what she was talking about.

"Have you forgotten you asked me to marry you?"

"Will you?" he replied with a thumping heart.

"Why wouldn't I? You make breakfast; you are handsome and really smart and are, no doubt, prepared to make me magnificent tailored suits and dresses."

They laughed and kissed and embraced each other until she pulled away.

"Seriously," she laughed, "our coffee is getting cold. We'll have to warm it up. But be careful and don't let it boil! It will ruin its flavor, and that's a bad omen, my papa says."

"You talk a lot about your father, I notice, less about your mother," Eugène observed.

"She is volatile and indifferent, coercive."

"Do you have anything good to say about her?"

"She is a well-mannered society lady—pretty, dresses well, and loves my father. I have an extended family we visit from time to time, especially during the holidays. I have younger cousins; we keep in touch and celebrate their birthdays together. I have an aunt Erna that I adore. She is the opposite of my mother. I ran away to her apartment whenever I could. I can tell you stories about grandparents, aunts, uncles, and cousins. Their lives will make you wonder about grace and horror. There are stories you want to remember forever, and others you want to bury."

"That's quite a tableau. As for me, I pledge to do anything in my power to fill our lives with love and understanding."

He embraced her; it was Saturday, and he had almost caught up with his work for the week. "Listen," he said, "I have a suggestion. Why don't you move in with me today? It will save you money," he suggested.

"Good idea," she agreed. "I'll pack my things and pay off my bill."

She came back mid-afternoon with two suitcases and made good use of a couple of small closets he'd cleared out for her. Someday they might be able to find a bigger apartment, he hoped.

For her part, Carmen had also fallen in love with Eugène at first sight. And what a sight he was. He looked like an exotic movie star,

PART ONE—EUGÈNE & CARMEN
CHAPTER EIGHT

or a Greek hero, at least according to her idea of how such men look: svelte, well proportioned, with dark, curly hair and warm, bright brown eyes. But he was even more than that. He had been kind and compassionate enough to sense her plight on that first cold night in the rue Elzévir. She would always remember that second evening, when she was lonely and tired of being afraid, she asked to sleep in his apartment. He was a perfect gentleman and made a bed for himself on the cutting table. No nightmares that night, nor the following one. Love and security prevailed.

And that was not all. She admired him for his vitality, his avid interest in books, politics, movies, sports, and entertainers. He was a well-rounded man with many interests, who also showed interest in her.

My mother and father were married within two months of their first meeting. They had a simple civil wedding at city hall, then a party given by my father's Hungarian friends. Their first dance was a czardas performed with speed and enthusiasm, then a second, and a third. Eugène could have danced all night. Carmen, on the other hand, never a night owl, not even on that special day, begged to leave before midnight.

Of course, my mother missed her family and her Nuremberg friends. She must have felt uprooted for months. There was no longer anyone with whom she could reminisce about her childhood. It had disintegrated from under her like porous stone.

Chapter Nine

Carmen and Eugène married in 1934. Their first child was born two years later. They called him Fred. They had seen the name on the marquee of a jewelry store in the rue Saint Honoré. It sounded very French, very classy to them. From the beginning, the work of caring for a baby left them ragged. Nighttime was especially difficult. Fred would cry his lungs out, and to calm him they would feed him again. Five minutes later he was raging and kicking his little legs. It was exhausting. Eugène had trouble getting up in the morning and caught himself dozing at his work. Then one day they noticed a bulge near the baby's groin and consulted a pediatrician. Their precious child had a hernia and would have to undergo an operation to repair it.

Eugène and Carmen went to the hospital where a nurse received them. She took Fred out of their arms and dressed him in a little green gown, then carried him to the operating room. Eugène thought Carmen would pass out from worry. It took great effort to stay calm, to reassure her. The operation was successful, and at last their baby began enjoying his sleep, as did they.

Carmen was a happy woman before the war. She loved children and flowers; she sang and laughed easily. The only thing Eugène wished he could change was her routinely early bedtime; he was just the opposite and never seemed to need much sleep. But Carmen didn't mind his going out in the evening without her. She was generous and urged him to continue enjoying the movies with Szego, who was always available. The next day at breakfast, he would tell her everything about the film he had seen: the title, the name of the actors, what the plot was about, as well as the outcome. He had seen so many movies in his life that he could say with confidence, and he said it often, that he knew all and any of the plots that past and present filmmakers have or will ever devise.

He regularly had early appointments with the clients who came to their apartment to try on their new garments. When they appeared, Carmen put Fred in his carriage and walked to the gardens at Place des Vosges, where she met other parents and their children. These frequent contacts enabled her to learn French rapidly. She felt at ease in her new land.

They were content together, and life would have been perfect, but for the worsening news coming out of Germany: Jewish citizens banned from their professions, forced sterilization, and death by gas for people who had mental problems or severe physical bodily infirmities. This was hard to believe. Their minds rebelled when confronting these horrors; there was no way to understand people who behaved so mercilessly. Hitler was a racist, a cunning demagogue, and a maniac. Many in his country were too cowed and frightened to protest his cruel policies.

Sadly, they learned that the Roman Catholic Church in Germany shamefully allied itself with the Reich when it signed a concordat with the criminal government, thereby ratifying the new racist laws. Yet some

PART ONE—EUGÈNE & CARMEN
CHAPTER NINE

courageous priests and lay people protested this decision. For its part, the Protestant Resistance bravely issued its opposition to Nazi politics. This gave the Grozingers a temporary warm feeling; there were still a few people in Germany who cared about the lives of others.

Notable among them were the young leaders of an underground group that called itself "The White Rose." During the war, they distributed thousands of leaflets protesting the wholesale elimination of categories of people judged undesirable by the Nazis. Sophie Scholl, her brother Henri, and their friends, mostly all students from the university of Munich, called for the active opposition of the German people against Nazi oppression and tyranny. They were the conscience of their country while thousands of their compatriots collaborated by means of their silence.

Meanwhile, things were happening in France. The French people had a new government led by the Socialist Léon Blum, who lost no time offering a revolutionary program. Le Front Populaire introduced reforms that struck everyone with a bang. It created the framework for a forty-hour workweek, and the addition of a two-week paid annual summer vacation.

The French were suddenly jumping from the Middle Ages to the Renaissance: collective bargaining, the extension of obligatory schooling, the opening of sports clubs. For the first time in the history of France, working people felt included. Several millions of them benefited from this generous legislation.

Eugène couldn't profit from any of these innovations because he was self-employed, but all the same, and as a consequence of these quasi-universal workers' gains, his business thrived as never before. There were new needs to be filled. Everyone wanted a taste of the seaside and the mountains. Overnight there was an increased demand for the knickers, summer jackets, cotton trousers, shorts, and skirts that were now in fashion. He prepared to fulfill these wishes by purchasing ample supplies of cloth in all sorts of colors to please a new clientele.

This turn of events made him think about his father. He praised his father's wisdom for having directed him toward a trade that nourished his household and made him useful to society. Unlike the poor Polish who worked in the coal mines of northern France in the worst conditions, ruining their lungs and often dying in darkness, no boss oppressed him or threatened to get rid of him by sending him back to his native country. His back might hurt from bending over the sewing machine, but his hands and face stayed clean. And while his fingers kept busy, his mind was free to listen to the radio. Thus he discovered a great generation of French singers: Yves Montand, Charles Aznavour, and Edith Piaf among them, whose songs Carmen and he learned by heart. Two among these artists, Aznavour and Montand, foreigners by birth, won the hearts of their listening public.

While some may point out that listening to songs and learning their lyrics is rather unimportant and somewhat frivolous, the songs brought them relief; songs were their poetry and elevated their minds. They needed music to erase their darkness, their fear for the future. They desperately wanted to be happy and live normal lives with family and friends in a progressive country at peace with the world.

Eugène was an ardent supporter of Prime Minister Léon Blum, the man of the moment who had brought progress and happiness to a large segment of the population. Here was a politician willing and able to change the status quo, who refused to send the police

PART ONE—EUGÈNE & CARMEN
CHAPTER NINE

to break workers' strikes, even when, in their fervor, they occupied factories and made their bosses prisoners. Instead of using force and repression, Blum helped mediate demands between the leaders of the strikers and their employers. The latter agreed to increase wages that had long been stagnant.

The prime minister was an open-minded democrat; he had been unafraid to ally his Socialist party to the Communist Left when the Right clamored for its exclusion. What struck an additional chord with Eugène was how calm and focused Léon Blum remained despite strident anti-Semitic jibes.

But the peace most French people yearned for was soon being compromised by outside events. Spain was in the throes of a violent civil war. General Franco and his fascist followers were waging war against the legitimately elected *Frente Popular* that, like Blum's government, emphasized work and peace. Naturally they asked their French brothers for help.

During the summer of 1936, Blum wanted to send warplanes over the Pyrenees to the Spanish resistance. But pressure from England forced him to ratify a nonintervention pact. What a joke! Eugène thought. The fascists were now completely free to use arms and men for the fight to the death in what would be a brutal civil war.

Eugène and Carmen's apartment became a busy meeting place. He could work and carry on animated conversations at the same time. Five or six friends came frequently; some in the morning, some in the afternoon, among them Szego, Kertes, Klein, and Struck. Sometimes Carmen joined them and made tea for everyone.

Maurice Struck had a brother in Toulouse who sent him *L'Express du Midi*, a reactionary, racist newspaper he read to understand the kind of indoctrination its readers adhered to. Maurice read the gathering an editorial whereby the Left was advised "to get used to the perspective of living surrounded by Hitler, Mussolini, and Franco."

This was the kind of language that delighted the ultra-Rightists. Eugène and his companions were stunned by these uncivil politics. How could people support the policies and practices of barbarians who killed, tortured, and enslaved? There was only one way to react against the threats, thought Eugène. If the time came to fight the enemy, he would join the ranks of the opposition.

In the meantime, they continued to take great pride in the prime minister. Léon Blum stood as the first Jewish prime minister ever elected to that post. Still, his detractors loathed him because of his origins. They tried to injure him by causing a vehicle collision, and when they pulled the prime minister out of his car, they beat him severely. Fortunately, he recovered and held office for the years 1936-37, but his trials were not over. After the German invasion of France, Maréchal Pétain, the eighty-two-year-old hero of World War I, had him arrested and tried for treason as well as for having weakened French forces. Despite the brilliant defense undertaken by Blum himself—he was a lawyer by profession—he was found guilty. Pétain had him jailed, and then handed him over to the occupying Nazis. They sent him to the concentration camps first at Buchenwald, then at Dachau. Allied troops rescued him in May 1945.

After his liberation, Blum would come back to politics and was elected again.

His allies wished only that he had intervened in the Spanish conflict.

PART ONE—EUGÈNE & CARMEN
CHAPTER NINE

He was not a timid person and could have made the difference in the conflagration that many foresaw as a rehearsal for a larger, more lethal confrontation with Hitler. French and English politics of peace at all costs made many people reconsider their loyalties.

Eugène's new hero was Maurice Thorez, the French Communist Party leader who allied himself with Moscow. He proposed the formation and organization of an international force of volunteers, who would assist and fight side by side with the legitimate Spanish government. In the meantime, Soviet Russia had given support to the Spanish Republicans.

Eugène was on fire and ready to enroll in the Brigades, but Carmen resisted this proposal with a force he didn't expect. For one thing, she hated Stalin, whom she denounced as a second Hitler.

"How can you trust a person who sacrifices some of his people for a so-called 'dictatorship of the proletariat'? Dictatorship! I don't like that word: to my ear it sounds like control and repression. No, I don't trust that Stalin; he'll mow over anyone who disagrees with him. Besides, we have a child whose happiness depends on us. I need you to help me raise our Fred."

As far as Eugène was concerned, he might as well have been a traitor to the just cause. Those who went to Spain to join the International Brigades came from all walks of life and numbered in the thousands. They served in medical units, as did the great American novelist Ernest Hemingway, and became soldiers in the fight against Franco and his forces. On the other hand, he would have betrayed Carmen and Fred if he had gone. So he remained in his atelier, glued to the radio, debating with his friends while thousands were putting their lives at risk.

Chapter Ten

When you live near a rumbling volcano, it is impossible to relax and go to bed at night. You listen to each sound with suspicion and dread. You eat fast and develop uncontrollable behaviors that prove to be deleterious to your health. Eugène began smoking habitually. Every time he lit up a cigarette, his nerves were soothed. But Carmen resented the smoke. She was ultra sensitive to smells and noises. "You are ruining your health, and mine," she warned when he began coughing.

One weekend, they took Fred to the Vincennes zoo. It was a radiant, cool spring day, but something seemed out of place. It was the lack of noise, an atmosphere of containment, restraint, and gravity, as when one expects some force of nature to ignite, but still hopes against hope it will go some other way. Eugène was lagging a little behind Carmen and Fred. He saw them heading away from the tiger compound. Suddenly he heard a piercing scream. It sounded like Carmen's voice, but distorted and amplified. A throng of people was gathering near the primates' exhibit. Fred had managed to fall into the monkey's cage. He was still holding the baby bottle he carried everywhere with him and was just picking himself up. He looked unharmed and unafraid as he watched the chattering chimpanzee coming toward him with outstretched arms. His parents held their breath, but unbelievably, in less than a second, everything was resolved. Fred handed his baby bottle to the chimp. The animal took it and turned around, uttering sounds of glee. Eugène jumped into the cage, swooped up his son, and handed him to Carmen. She sobbed with relief while Fred howled for his bottle.

The incident frightened Eugène. It kept replaying in his mind, then gave way to mixed emotions. Peace, he thought, may often prevail when goodwill is at work. People and politicians can bring it about, rev it like an engine and succeed. That not quite three-year-old son of his knew what to do when he held out his small hand; in turn, the chimp reached out with its own and sealed the offer. Faith and candor had won that day.

Before his son's birth, Eugène's concept of family was vague. Now he was devoted to the idea that family comes first, but the idea that his small clan's security was anything but guaranteed made him exceedingly anxious. Menacing global forces were gathering. Unforeseen catastrophes were imminent. He decided to listen to Carmen and give up smoking cigarettes.

Carmen's brother, Maurice, had recently been living in Strasbourg, still French territory, managing the French branch of a German company that manufactured sports equipment, such as soccer balls, horseriding saddles, bridles, and other sundry leather accoutrements. He derived great pleasure from this position. He was himself a good athlete, a lover of sports. He and Eugène got on famously; it helped that both were soccer fanatics. They would have talked about teams and individual players all day long if Carmen hadn't intervened.

PART ONE—EUGÈNE & CARMEN
CHAPTER TEN

This was Maurice's first visit to Paris. He was only staying for the weekend, and Carmen wanted to have him for herself. She made arrangements to have Fred play with the child of a close friend, and woke her brother early in the morning. They had breakfast in a café, and then decided to visit ancient Les Halles, that so-called *ventre de Paris*, the belly of Paris, memorialized by the writer Émile Zola. It was a wholesale food market filled with produce, fish, meat, vegetables, fruit and cheese, which arrived at Les Halles from every part of France in the early morning hours and overflowed into the extra modern Baltard Pavilions.

The place was bustling with people carrying, displaying, bartering, buying, and selling their goods, shouting to one another, whistling and singing, going in and out of the intriguing pavilions entirely built from cast iron metal and glass.

The market exuded a mélange of aromas, mostly pleasant, that became sharper as the morning progressed, and as the refuse piled up. Great buckets of water were flung to dispel the most offensive odors of decay. Yet in the debris, some bruised apples here, there a random box of cabbages, and some perfectly good potatoes remained. It didn't take long for the hungry to gather those remnants.

Maurice and Carmen sat in a restaurant nearby to eat the fare of the people who worked in Les Halles. The most famous dish, a delicious *soupe à l'oignon*, melted on the tongue and warmed them.

From there it was a short walk to the Louvre. Carmen warned her brother that they could explore only a small area of the immense museum. "You cannot visit the Louvre in the course of a day. So you'll have to come back to see us many more times."

They entered the edifice off the rue du Louvre, using *La Cour Carrée*, the heart of the old Renaissance palace, so called for its perfect symmetry. They sat on a bench, and from that vista they gazed at the remarkable sculptures.

"Let's go inside," Maurice said, "I want to see the *Mona Lisa*."

"Relax, we'll get there. We're in no hurry. I often come here with Fred. He runs around and feeds the pigeons. Isn't this a wonderful place? Imagine the people who walked here two centuries ago. I hope it was peacetime, and spring, that the sun shone, hot enough to warm their limbs; that they sat right where we are to admire their surroundings. Wouldn't that have been a good time?"

"And what kind of time is it for us, sister?"

She wasn't ready to predict, dared not. History would tell thereafter what they were about to live through.

They went to the Eiffel Tower, craned their necks at the three hundred meter-high structure, and stared at the sight of its elephantine feet. Then they took the metro back to the Place des Vosges. There they sat down in Carmen's favorite café, the one at the angle of the square where one could sit down to sip hot chocolate.

"A beautiful city," said Maurice. "I wish I could live here."

"Why not? I would be so thrilled if you could," she replied.

The day was passing fast. They reminisced about their lives when they were the only two children in their parents' household, when he, the oldest, her favorite person in the whole world, took care of her while her mother went out and glittered.

"The belle of Nuremberg!" they exclaimed together, laughing.

Maurice had a girlfriend. He was raising a son. He had just told

PART ONE—EUGÈNE & CARMEN
CHAPTER TEN

his parents, who weren't pleased to hear that their son had skipped both the engagement and the wedding ceremony. He had wanted his sister to be the first to know about the child, but he had not then been able to find out where Carmen was.

"You know, Maurice, I decided to run away from home on the spur of the moment. I was going to write you when I got to Paris, but then I met Eugène, and my past history evaporated. I was overwhelmed. So much happened all at once; forgive me for not sending our address earlier. I am so happy you came, but let's talk about you. What is your girlfriend's name, what is she like?"

"Lena comes from a very modest background."

"But you love her. So who cares? Tell me about the baby. What's his name?"

"Hector. He is two months old."

"Hector? What kind of name is that?"

"You know, Homer's *Iliad*. I used to read it to you. Hector was always my favorite character because he loved peace and would have preferred to stay home with his family. But when war caught up with him, he showed great courage. Hector seemed like a perfect name for this child I brought into the world at such a time."

"Ah, yes, but what about Lena? Tell me more about her."

Maurice closed his eyes, apparently struggling to think what to say about her.

"That's just it, there isn't much to say about Lena. I told you, she is a simple person." He opened his eyes wide, refocusing. "Well, I might as well tell you everything. Lena was my cleaning lady. She stayed late one night. We lost our heads. What can I say? It just happened. She doesn't want to keep the child. All the better for me! I take full responsibility."

Maurice did not want to marry Lena any more than she wanted to marry him. There was too much difference in their backgrounds. She had very little schooling, except that given by her assiduously Catholic and church-going family, who had no love for Jews.

"How can you live with an anti-Semite?" Carmen asked, alarmed.

"We've gone our separate ways. She doesn't want to have anything to do Hector. He is mine to keep."

"Oh, Maurice, I am so sorry."

Maurice allowed Carmen to hug him, but soon shook her off with good-humored laughter.

"There is nothing to be sad about. We make mistakes. But in this case, even if he is just an infant, Hector is definitely not a mistake. He's my pride and joy, the best thing that could have happened to me. I have been lucky my entire life; I've a career I enjoy, good friends in Strasbourg, a great family, and you, my favorite, my darling sister, and now this child who has given me a special hold on life, a purpose, the direction I've always lacked. He's delightful. You should see him! I know I'm a little bit too proud. He's got my voice, a good strong one, and my hands, my big feet, and my ears. I'm sure he'll take to sports easily. He coos and kicks his legs in tempo with the music I play."

"Poor Maurice," she teased, "you can't even carry a tune."

"Come on now. I'm not so bad. At any rate, he loves the sound of my voice. It comforts him."

"Do you have a photo?"

"Yes, of course, take a look at my little prince."

"Your portrait!" Carmen exclaimed. "All these curls, and the

PART ONE—EUGÈNE & CARMEN
CHAPTER TEN

laughing eyes. He is a second you."

Maurice laughed with satisfaction.

"Yes, I told you, no one can deny our relationship, and I daresay I am a good father."

"Remember how I took care of you when our mother traveled? You were almost as cute as my Hector. Just joking! You were adorable, and now you're grown up and more lovely than ever."

They hugged each other; then Maurice returned to what was now his favorite subject.

"I considered everything carefully. I went to City Hall with Lena and had myself declared as his father. He was duly registered, Hector Tieme, son of Maurice Tieme. Lena has agreed to nurse him for a while. It's a good thing for babies, I've been told."

"How motherly of her!"

"I pay her for doing it. It's better that way. I wouldn't like for us to fight over the child. I've found a good woman to keep him while I work."

Her beloved brother! Carmen and Eugène accompanied Maurice to Gare de L'Est on the day he returned to Strasbourg. They promised they would go greet their new nephew as soon as possible.

But Maurice never reached home, never saw his child again. The circumstances were somewhat murky. He had gotten into a fight on the train. Three men had beaten him brutally; he suffered fatal head trauma. He was dead when the train reached its destination. The murderers vanished. No witnesses came forward.

Carmen grieved for months. Nothing could cheer her. Maurice would live in her mind as long as she was alive. Without him the brightest day grew cloudy. She missed him, mourned for him daily.

She soon heard from her parents. Her brother's death was a devastating blow. They imagined all sorts of scenarios, most of them having to do with Maurice being a Jew. They thought that the murderers intended to have their fun with him, to put him in his place, to teach him a lesson for being what he was.

The death of their older son shattered Carmen's parents' last hopes for a safe life in Germany. They had run a successful business in sharpening stones, and owned three warehouses in Nuremberg, bought earlier with Berta's mother's inheritance. They left everything behind, though her father hoped to revive his business some day, if on a more modest scale. In the meantime, Switzerland seemed an ideal place for relocation. Berta's mother had been born and educated there. Berta was still a citizen of Switzerland, and she would fight tooth and nail to negotiate entry for her husband, Sonia, and for Ferry, her last child, born as she was nearing fifty. Meanwhile, Carmen's father and Sonia, her younger sister, were both coming to France. Eugène and Carmen made ready to welcome them.

Chapter Eleven

Berta was a seasoned traveler, an expert saleswoman who helped her husband in all facets of their business. She was used to traveling first class, but she felt lucky to find a seat in the less desirable second-class area on the train bound for Zurich.

No one ever expects to be forced out of his or her country. Friends and relatives are there, and dwellings are rendered comfortable as well as aesthetically pleasing through years of updating and embellishments. There are symphonies to attend and museums to visit, art to become acquainted with, and movie theaters in which to see films and plays; also, favorite restaurants and shopping areas, and unique places not to be found elsewhere. Leaving a country under duress is like leaving the world.

Berta had never been a sentimental person. She could be harsh with her words; Carmen knew that first hand. For the moment, she was a vagabond who had lost her eldest child, her favorite, her Maurice, the only one of her children who understood and knew how to assuage her easily erupting temper and turn it into grumbling laughter. And now he was dead, killed not in Germany, where people disappeared, and lifeless and tortured bodies turned up in ditches, but in France, a country without a *Führer*, where freedoms could still be enjoyed by most.

She didn't know she could shed so many bitter tears without exhausting the source of their welling. And then there was the matter of this illegitimate grandson. Sol, engulfed in his emotions of loss, refused to talk about the matter. "Later," he said; it was no use trying to change his mind. Despite their disagreements, Carmen felt for her mother and was ready to help any way she could.

Berta had stayed in contact with childhood friends who still lived in Zurich, among them Anna and Emil Finkelkraut, both lawyers, with whom she would be staying. They promised to use their legal skills to help her and the rest of her family obtain refuge in their native land.

They were waiting for her at the train station. Berta found them craning their necks in the midst of cohorts. An aura of malaise seemed to envelop those who had just arrived from Germany. How many, like herself, were fleeing a totalitarian country they justly feared?

First, Anna and Emil had reminisced with Berta about their childhood together. Anna hoped that would help distract Berta from her pain, at least for a while.

The two women bonded early in kindergarten and continued their relationship through high school. Anna, first in her graduating class, had gone on to university, while Berta left for London, where she married Carmen's father.

"You were a rebellious one, and so sure of yourself," Anna recalled. "You could easily have gone to university to become a doctor, perhaps a psychiatrist."

"Maybe . . . why not?" Berta replied. "But I was in love, and I wanted to get away from my mother, who was all rules and dedication to her charities."

PART ONE—EUGÈNE & CARMEN
CHAPTER ELEVEN

Anna looked at her husband over dinner. She raised her hand slightly to signal it was time to change the conversation and distract her friend away from fresh sorrow.

"Let's have coffee on the veranda," she proposed. "The view of the mountains is spectacular."

"Impressive," Berta responded. "If only they provided a refuge for my family."

"And how is Erna?" Anna asked. "I always marveled that you two were sisters. You are so different."

"Erna is married to a musician who plays with the Richard Strauss orchestra. Theo is not Jewish, and no one knows Erna is. She is very lucky. Strauss has hired her to manage the orchestra's wardrobe during their upcoming performances abroad. Otherwise, she's the same quiet, effaced person she has always been. She'll survive—no one will ever notice her."

Berta took another sip of her coffee. "Apropos," she said, "that Strauss is a fearless individual. He accepted the public's applause at the end of a performance, but pointedly avoided making the Nazi salute when Hitler rose."

"Does Erna have children?" Anna asked Berta.

"No, no children, though they wish they had some. But my sister with her quiet looks has managed to do everything she can to lure Carmen away from me. She invited her to stay with her for weeks on end, depriving me of much needed help. I'm sure it was she who encouraged Carmen to pursue her half-baked dreams. I blame her for my daughter running away to Paris."

"Doesn't everyone feel the need to run away from their parent at some point, Berta? At least now she is happy and safe. She just preceded you and the rest of your family out of Germany; that must console you," observed Anna.

"Perhaps, but a daughter has a duty to stand by her family. Carmen deliberately cut herself off from us. She is a stubborn and egotistical girl who did not even consult us about getting married to some wild Hungarian!"

There was a pause and a heavy silence. Berta had written Anna about Maurice's sad demise. There was no need to bring it up. A genuine *cri du coeur* pushed Anna out of her chair toward Berta. She wrapped her arms around her friend's shoulders.

"Let go, dear Berta! I know what you are going through. What happened can't be undone. You still have two children to raise, and family and friends."

The proud Berta began to sob. Anna thought it must have been the first time she crumbled in the presence of another person.

"Right now, I wish I could think only about my oldest son," Berta wept. "How can I mourn properly when storms rage around us? It's too much for me. They're killing people in Germany. They have concentration camps there. They take people without warning. For what reason, what have they done? A lot of them are Jewish—is that a crime? And my Maurice, what did he do to deserve death at such a young age?" Berta did not expect Anna and Emil to answer her questions. She was lost in her grief.

What was the truth about these reports? Anna and Emil felt for their friend and, at the same time, marveled at their good fortune. Switzerland was neutral. Its citizens could go to bed at night without having to fear what might take place the next day.

Chapter Twelve

Maurice's Strasbourg friends made arrangements for the funeral. Carmen took the train alone, having convinced Eugène she preferred it that way. Berta wired that she felt unwell and could not travel. Her father and Sonia were to meet her at the train station in Strasbourg.

Retracing her brother's last voyage was an all-absorbing, pain-filled task. She was unable to interact with anyone, even in the most trivial way, and refused to make contact with the travelers seated next to her. The woman sitting directly across from her offered a piece of candy. An elderly gentleman picked up the handkerchief she dropped and asked if she was all right. Could he help the lovely young lady in any way, he asked? She shook her head and looked elsewhere. Perhaps this man was kind, but would he have helped Maurice in his time of need? Would he have alerted the ticket master, or testified against the murderers?

The train stopped in several smaller cities, making the trip interminable. In her haste to leave Paris, she had not thought to take any food along. She was hungry, but the idea of eating made her nauseated. She fell into a restless sleep, the kind that makes you believe that you are awake and leaves you groggy. She awoke with a jolt in the Strasbourg train station and wondered what she was doing there.

Someone knocked at the window. She thought she heard voices calling her name; she got up like an automaton and sought the purse and the light bag she had hastily packed. A shape among the crowd of travelers materialized near her.

Her father enclosed her in his arms. They were joined by Sonia and embraced until they had no tears left to shed. At last Sol hailed a cab that took them to the Jewish cemetery situated in a poor neighborhood lacking trees and grace. Broken tombstones lay on the ground, and unsightly weeds everywhere spoke more about neglect than about eternal peace.

A group of people surrounded the fresh gash in the earth where Maurice would lay. Ensconced in her grief, Carmen paid no attention to the other mourners. Presently the burial ceremony began. A rabbi evoked Maurice's achievements, his love of sports, and his brilliant career. His friends and business associates came forward and praised him one by one, but no one related the circumstances that had caused his death as requested by his father.

The casket was lowered, and the ancient Aramaic prayer was intoned, "*Yiskadol v'yiskadosh shmey rabbo.*"

Then Sonia, Sol, and Carmen, followed by the rest of the mourners, threw a spade of dirt on the grave, a last act of kindness toward the deceased.

When all was done the rabbi announced the luncheon that was to follow. "All those who wish to come are invited," announced the rabbi.

"Do we have to go, Papa?" Carmen asked.

"Yes, we should make an appearance. We won't stay long. We need to catch an early train back to Paris."

PART ONE—EUGÈNE & CARMEN
CHAPTER TWELVE

She turned around to take a last look at her brother's grave, and as she did, her eye caught the figure of a young woman carrying an infant. Lena and Hector, she thought. She called out their names, but in her state of grief, she couldn't be sure she had seen them. Like a vision, they had vanished. New tears welled up. She returned to Maurice's grave. She wanted to tell him that she regretted deeply not meeting baby Hector and Lena. She would have persuaded Lena to let her raise her nephew along with her Fred. She murmured, "Forgive me, dear brother."

Sol had endeavored to find Lena before leaving Germany. He'd hired a private investigator to search for her, with no results. In the turmoil of impending war, with people scattering far and wide, it was a demanding task to locate a mother who had fled with her infant.

Sol and Sonia returned to Paris with Carmen. They stayed in mourning for a week according to the Jewish custom. Eugène shared the pain of his wife's family in a state of complete helplessness. He could not stay in place for a minute. He wanted to hold and kiss his wife to help relieve her grief, if only in a small way. She was unresponsive, not aware of anyone else, not even of her little son. She had built a wall around herself. Eugène admitted to himself that he was relieved to have work during that time, an excuse to retire with his needles and his sewing machine. Szego, that good friend, came to bring food for the company after his workday was done. They spent some time quietly discussing things in Hungarian.

Eugène came to like Carmen's father a great deal over the next two years they were in contact. Sol brimmed with energy. For all his troubles, the death of his son and a hurried exile from a country he'd considered his own, he managed the strength to cheer his family. "We are together and that is the most important thing," he'd say. "Furthermore, all of us are working to build a better future for ourselves."

Sonia and Sol departed when the traditional week of grieving came to an end; the girl for Switzerland to rejoin her mother, Sol to a rented apartment in Saint Louis, just across the French border from his family. In spite of the collective efforts of Berta and her friends, he was denied safe haven in Switzerland.

Carmen, Eugène, and Fred made the trip to Saint Louis a few times. On these occasions, Berta, Sonia, and toddler Ferry also joined them. During these visits, Eugène began to understand Carmen's mixed feelings toward her mother. Berta was a cantankerous woman whose mood turned as readily as a weathervane. She could be aggressive and cutting in her remarks, especially those she directed at her daughter's husband, even though he tried hard to win her over.

On one such trip, he had made two skirts out of a silky fabric, one each for Berta and Sonia. He presented them to his mother-in-law, who took them without a word and threw them on a chair with a look of disdain.

"Do you not like them?" he asked as politely as he could.

"Who would? One of them is too long and the other too short," she answered in a scornful voice.

"I'm sorry, but younger women can afford to show a bit more of their legs, so I thought you would like something that looks more classical," Eugène replied tentatively.

"Classical?" she sneered. "You call that classical? Perhaps for a gypsy but not for a lady, and certainly not for Sonia!"

PART ONE—EUGÈNE & CARMEN
CHAPTER TWELVE

Carmen caught her husband's eye with a look that clearly intimated to say nothing more. He relented, and his face darkened. Sol made no comment. The tick-tock of the cuckoo clock grew louder in the suffocating silence that engulfed the room. Then Sonia made her entrance and broke the spell. "Is that skirt for me?" she asked. She wrapped it around herself with a half turn of her body and exclaimed, "Doesn't it look well on me? I love it."

Indeed, it suited her. She was a slender but big-boned teenager, the kind who tends to gain weight with age. For the moment, she was aglow with the freshness of youth, with gleaming brown eyes and tightly curled black hair, a sharp contrast to Carmen's blonde, green-eyed looks.

Sol looked at her proudly.

"You look absolutely splendid!" He pulled Sonia into his arms with a hug and a kiss, and thanked Carmen and Eugène warmly for their gifts to his family. No one said anything about Berta's conduct. Eugène was still expecting some kind of apology from his mother-in-law. None came, but he was cheered and thankful for the enthusiasm exhibited by both father and daughter.

They hadn't brought anything for Sol but had not forgotten him. They decided a suit would likely please him, but Eugène needed to take Sol's measurements for a perfect fit. He was quite a dandy and, though short in stature, possessed a natural elegance. Whatever he wore, casual or dressy, appeared made-to-order, down to his socks and shoes.

The rapid flight of the Tieme family from Germany required them to travel as lightly as possible. They had not carried much luggage; indeed they could not give any hint they were fleeing the country. Their furniture and most of their possessions had been left behind, so Sol was delighted by the offer of a new suit to add to his depleted wardrobe.

The rest of the visit was pleasant enough. They went out for a walk in the woods that surrounded tiny Saint Louis and returned in time for a nice meal, prepared by none other than Berta, who was an excellent cook. They thanked her politely, and she smiled in return. Her thunder had passed. She was definitely a strange one.

The goodbyes with Sonia were affectionate. Carmen hugged her father and showered him with many kisses, then resignedly deposited a peck on her mother's cheek.

"She treated you that way to humiliate me, to punish me for having run away," said Carmen during the train ride home to Paris. "She's a bully and a coward. She could have talked to me directly. I would have been happy to answer her questions. She knows damn well what prompted my escape: pulling me out of high school at fifteen, making me her maid!"

She raged, and Eugène held her hand. What could he say? This mother and daughter would not be able to forgive one another, any more than Berta and her own mother had in their time.

Chapter Thirteen

How is it that we keep transmitting patterns of relationships, good and bad, from one generation to the next without even being aware of it? And, more importantly, how can we prevent the passing of our own negative behaviors to our progeny? It takes effort and willingness to look objectively at oneself and examine one's motivation and conduct. We can choose not to repeat the parental behaviors that made us suffer and avoid inflicting them on our own children. After all, we are not mere acorns who fall close to the tree, but human beings endowed with brains and free will. And might not a passion for better relations within the family circle even influence and move along the goodwill of humanity itself?

The way we deal with others often corresponds to a false perception of what we imagine they are. All these stereotypes: Italians are excitable, the British are stiff, Americans are big children, Jews are money hungry, Germans are pushy.

I know, sometimes I philosophize because I yearn for universal peace. Like others, my family deserved to be treated fairly; neither as aliens who must be incarcerated, nor as objects to burn and dispose of.

If Eugène had believed in God, he would first say that all people are God's children; therefore all of them should be allowed to breathe

the fresh air in peace. But he did not believe in God, and he lived only in the reality of the moment, however irrational that may seem. In this moment of the late 1930s, the world had gone mad. Nazis wanted to exterminate his loved ones, and millions of others were condemned as undesirable—his brothers and sisters, experiencing unmerited and uncommon deprivations, degradations, and deaths.

"We are here," he said, "and it is here in this chaos that we exist and resist or cease to be."

One day, Eugène received a visit from a police officer. Did he know a Sol Tieme, a German citizen who lived in Saint Louis and often traveled between Paris and Strasbourg? For what reason did the wife and daughter live in Switzerland while the father lived in France?

The police suspected the entire family of being spies. Fortunately, Carmen was out shopping. She would have been terrified to hear that her parents were under suspicion. Eugène forced himself to remain calm while informing the policeman.

"Yes, officer," he said politely, "I know Mr. Tieme. He is my father-in-law, a refugee from Nazi Germany. His wife is a Swiss citizen who has resettled in Zurich for safety's sake. Unfortunately, he himself has not been able to obtain a visa from the Swiss, but has temporary papers to live in Saint Louis. He does travel on occasion to Paris and Strasbourg for business purposes, and also to visit my wife, who is his daughter. Like many of us, he is just trying to survive in difficult circumstances."

"And what kind of business does he do?"

"He buys and sells sharpening stones."

"The authorities in Saint Louis asked us to investigate. Doesn't

PART ONE—EUGÈNE & CARMEN
CHAPTER THIRTEEN

he know that it is the law for resident aliens to report to the local police as soon as they set foot in France? By the way, may I see your identity papers?"

Eugène kept them in a locked drawer. He got them out and let the policeman see them without protest or fear. The latter examined them and nodded. "Everything is in order. But you understand that your testimony about Mr. Tieme is binding. We have him under surveillance and might have occasion to speak to you again."

This visit had not pleased Eugène at all. To be known by the police is never a good sign, especially when you yourself are a recent immigrant. He couldn't afford to hide the event from Carmen. They lost no time in alerting her parents.

It had proven too difficult and too dangerous for Sol and Berta's family to live separately in two different countries. Sol was not about to remain where he was not wanted. He and Berta decided to move to Italy where foreigners in possession of valid identity papers could obtain residency.

Sol acted fast. He contacted an old acquaintance, an Italian citizen who lived in Milan. The latter agreed to become his partner in the sharpening stone business. But despite his best efforts, after a year of setbacks, Sol gave up and sold the business for half of its value. If not for Sonia, who quit school to become a waitress in a bar, the family would have starved. After much debate, Sol decided to contact his sister, Bella, who had emigrated from Germany to the United States with her husband to escape poverty a long time before the war. Now past middle age, they were well established in Dallas, Texas, where they reported, "the sun always shone." They were eager to help and agreed to sponsor their desperate relatives.

Prompted by the imminent departure of her family to the U.S., Carmen decided to visit her parents in Milan as soon as possible. She had a presentiment this might be her last opportunity to see them for years to come. She was bringing them some clothing for their six-day passage across the Atlantic. It was the beginning of a cold winter, and she wanted them to keep warm on the ship.

Ferry Tieme, her much younger brother, barely older than her son, Fred, was about to embark on a voyage that would take him far from his European roots. He later Americanized his name, becoming "Fred Time." Uncle Fred's looks were all his own. In photographs of the two Freds posed together, in fact, he resembled neither Sol nor Berta, while Carmen's Fred looked so much like Maurice he could have easily passed for theirs.

Not everyone in the family was eager to leave Europe. Sonia was broken-hearted. She had been lucky to find a job in a café, but she found that working suited her, and she sometimes preferred it to being at home. "When I'm done with work I go home and have to help my mother with cooking and cleaning," she complained, "and now we're leaving for America."

"I don't want to go, I have a boyfriend, Angelo. I love him; I want to stay with him here in Italy, but Father and Mother won't let me. They both say it would not be proper, that I am still too young to make that kind of decision. They're old; they don't understand. It's all about great opportunities in the United States for them. I have no say."

Sonia sobbed. Nobody could stop her tears. She was only seventeen, in love with a boy she had no hope of seeing again, uprooted for the third time. Nothing made sense as she faced the unknown. Once more she would arrive in a foreign country and be forced to learn to speak another language. She would not have any friends, no one to talk to.

Carmen kissed and hugged her. "Why, you didn't have any problem learning Italian. You are smart and friendly. You'll see everything will be fine." Carmen smiled, but she understood her sister's tears all too well. She knew the pull of staying with the man you love, and she remembered the temptation of freedom from Berta's domineering household. She smoothed Sonia's hair.

It would be twenty-five years before she would see her parents, Ferry, or Sonia again.

Chapter Fourteen

Eugène never forgot the day he met Arthur Koestler. He would not know until after the war how famous a writer this man would become. Koestler came to Eugène's home in rue des Tournelles during the last days of 1938, at a time when terrible events were being strung rapidly, one after another in an interminable series, like beads on a growing chain.

Arthur Koestler knocked at his door, introduced himself, and came in drenched from the downpour that caught him on the way to the apartment, which doubled as a workshop. Eugène offered him a towel and a cup of tea. Koestler needed a new suit, he explained, to replace the worn-out corduroy he wore.

"The only one I own," he added with a wry smile.

He was a man of average height, with very dark hair and a prominent nose, self-assured, perhaps a little cocky, with a magnetic personality that helped him look charming and even handsome.

"Frieda from the Hungarian club gave me your name," he declared. "She says you are a magnificent tailor who will turn me into a gentleman again."

Eugène noticed he had a slightly noticeable but familiar accent. He couldn't help asking, "Are you Hungarian?"

"Yes, but I've traveled and lived in a few other countries, and learned other languages as well. However, I was born in Budapest; my early schooling was in Austria. Compliments on your fine ear. People don't usually recognize my Hungarian undertones. What about you?"

"I lived in Budapest for only a few weeks. I come from a very small village. No one has ever heard of it, except for my brother, Elias. Honorable countryman, let me ask. Is this new suit meant for a special occasion?"

"You might say that. I need something that can look presentable and stylish. Perhaps you could find a handsome but reasonably priced fabric for me. Right now I am low on funds. I don't mind telling you, my last few years have been most chaotic. Let's just say that I've been on the go, at times fleeing the powers that be, at times being imprisoned and even under sentence of death. I want to face whatever comes next honestly clothed and shod," he laughed with good humor.

Eugène looked at his client's feet. His shoes were indeed fatigued. They reminded him of the ones Charlie Chaplin's famous little tramp wears and then eats when famished.

"And where will you be going next, may I ask?"

"I'd like to get as close as possible to the shores of England," he responded with a large smile.

Eugène was intrigued by the fellow, avidly curious to know where he had been and what he had seen and done. But he was perceptive enough to notice a shadow cross his new client's face and refrained from asking more questions. Instead, they agreed about the color of his future garment, a midnight blue fabric he had bought in bulk. Eugène took his client's measurements and announced, "The fitting is in five days."

PART ONE—EUGÈNE & CARMEN
CHAPTER FOURTEEN

In the meantime, he took a break to go to the Hungarian club to find out all he could about the man. Frieda didn't know much about this Mr. Koestler. A friend of hers had introduced them. She said the man was there to play cards; during the course of the game he asked if she knew a tailor.

Eugène told Carmen about his new client. He was a man about his age and seemed to be extremely intelligent. He couldn't wait until Koestler returned.

"I'm very curious about the life he's led," he said.

His wife wasn't convinced he should pry. "Don't you think it's rude to ask him questions? Anyway, what does it matter? The important thing is that he pays you for your work."

One of them had to keep a level head, and that was fine with him. However, in spite of his wife's advice, while working on Koestler's suit he constructed a whole life story for his intriguing client. Hadn't Koestler said he'd been imprisoned in Spain? He had fought against Franco for the cause; Eugène respected that. And what about England? Was he a spy in her pay? He might also be a turncoat who had abjured his beliefs in Communism.

Koestler returned exactly on the day and time they had set, still wearing his washed-up corduroys, but sporting a new shirt and new shoes. Again Eugène offered him some tea and was frank to allow that he found him sympathetic. Koestler replied to that outburst with a warm smile. Eugène seized this opportunity to ask him more questions.

Would Koestler confide why he wanted to go to England? It was a country he himself didn't have much sympathy for.

"Wasn't it England who forced Blum's government into submission, thereby nullifying his intervention on behalf of the Republicans against the fascist Franco?" Eugène asked.

"You're right, it was England," replied Koestler calmly after a sip of his tea. "That decision turned out to be a costly mistake for all of Europe."

"But nonintervention gave a signal to Franco. It let him know that he could do away with democracy without restraint. On account of that, the International Brigades were ordered to withdraw. So now Franco is completely free to hound and kill his remaining adversaries. Spain will become one more dictatorship," Eugène insisted.

"Forget it, that battle is already past," shrugged his client. "Nothing can be done about that. The present fight is against Germany. There's but one political faction there, the Nazis, who would make us believe they face only one enemy: Jews, whose only crime is to exist."

"*Kristallnacht*," Eugène said, nodding. "Are you Jewish?"

"I must be if we agree to believe that only Jews worry about Jews. The unfortunate Herschel Grynszpan didn't foresee that his shooting Vom Rath would lead to even more consequences than that of broken glass."

"Yes because he was avenging his parents! Unfortunately his action gave Hitler and his cronies the opportunity to engineer a massive retaliation against any perceived enemy of the Reich. I think the world is not sufficiently alarmed. We need to stop that madman."

"Why does he despise us so? At times I can't even believe this is happening. We're caught in this crazy fairy tale, like Bluebeard's wives. When will the civilized world react?" Eugène asked.

PART ONE—EUGÈNE & CARMEN
CHAPTER FOURTEEN

"The civilized world no longer exists, my friend. It's caught a virus and has succumbed. Look at France, a vaunted land of refuge, yes? Welcoming the refugees from Germany? No! Offering a haven to the Spaniards who survived the Spanish Civil War? The answer is still no. No welcome band, no banquet for these valiant fighters. They were sent to the Vernet internment camp, that stinking piece of trash, stuck in the otherwise lovely foothills of the Pyrenees. The vermin-infested collection of ramshackle huts where they spend their days are open to winds and rain. Food is scarce and of poor quality. People catch infections and diseases of all kinds, and those who were already weakened by months of hard fighting die from neglect."

"I know all this first hand. I was interned there. I probably deserved the treatment I received because in addition to being a foreigner, and a former prisoner of the Fascist Franco regime, I am also an ex-communist and a Jew."

Eugène was shaken to learn this; the official line was that refugees from Spain were welcomed by the French government and treated like guests.

"And you managed to escape Franco's jails?" he asked.

Koestler smiled. "I had to. I was under a death sentence! Then I arrived in Vernet and understood once more that I had no other choice but to escape again. So I did. I'm becoming good at this game."

He lit a cigarette and sent circles of smoke in the air. His pose was nonchalant, though he seemed like a tough, invincible man of action. Eugène hoped Koestler would tell his entire life story, especially why he was no longer a communist.

For his part, Eugène still thought that Communism was the only ideology worth fighting for. It offered hope and care to the downtrodden, and its adherents had proven their commitment by the many who bravely responded to the call to go to Spain to help the resistance fight Franco and his allies.

"I have many friends in England," Koestler said softly. "They assure me that foreigners who reside there have the right to partake of everyday life freely, just like any British-born citizen. I have traveled enough and paid my dues to important causes, some of which I now deem to be mere idolatries! To sum up, I need a rest in a country where I can be ordinary, at least for the time being."

They sat in silence for a moment. Then Koestler tried on his suit. He thanked his compatriot, then embraced him and wished him well. He lit a cigarette before going outside. Eugène opened the door, and Koestler disappeared in a cloud of smoke.

After the war Eugène read an article about Koestler in *Paris Soir*. He learned that his client was a famous writer, who had written a best-seller called *Darkness at Noon*.

Eugène read that book during his captivity; it belonged to a buddy of his, a fellow internee, a well-educated Jew, his friend Marcel, who helped him in his darkest moments. Cleaning his bookshelves many years later, Eugène's eye fell upon that same tattered copy of *Darkness at Noon*. He realized he had not given it back to Marcel, or perhaps his buddy had made the book a gift. He found the book riveting, though too anti-communist for his liking.

Persecution and crime, even in the name of a promising ideology, are egregious and inimical to the progress of society. That's what Rubashov, the main protagonist of *Darkness at Noon*, comes to understand during his incarceration. He is a member of the Bolshevik Party and participates in the October Revolution. Later he exercises power like a good communist; that is, he is instrumental in the persecution of others. Suddenly he is thrown in prison on Stalin's orders. He's been accused of having followed "sentimental impulses," and finds himself in contradiction with "historical necessity."

In the end, Rubashov's only choice is to act like a *mensch*, to admit that he has committed a crime, but not the one his tormentors want him to acknowledge. Like a good *apparatchik* he backed the party line and went along with the directive to starve the peasants by confiscating the seeds that produce food. Who in his right mind would believe such an action to be part of a design intended to better the future of the masses? Does "historical necessity" require the arbitrary death of certain classes of citizens?

"The end justifies the means is a crude lie," said our man to his tormentors. One night invisible goons garrote him in his dark cell.

Koestler escaped from the Soviet Union after having been an ardent supporter of Communism. He already knew what it took so long for Eugène to admit: that Stalin was as much the thug and the murderer Hitler proved to be.

When war came to France, Arthur Koestler was still on its soil. He briefly joined the French Legion and then soon defected from it. Thereafter he reached England, the land of his dreams, and became a British citizen. Eugène never encountered him again.

Chapter Fifteen

In 1939 Hitler and Stalin signed a pact of nonaggression. It guaranteed the neutrality of the Soviet Union in the eventuality of armed conflict. This disappointing and evil entente allowed Hitler freedom to operate in Western and Eastern Europe, and enabled Stalin to establish his own zone of influence. Germany invaded Poland on September 1; the Red Army entered and occupied Vilna and Danzig soon after. For the French, mobilization became a certainty.

These events shocked the like-minded friends of Eugène and Carmen. They had been so credulous about Hitler. His *bête noire* were the Jews. Germany, he said, must be "Judenrein." The German Jewish population would be eliminated through drastic measures including torture and murder. Eugène could not believe that Stalin would get into bed with Hitler. He was so naïve, then, like a person walking with eyes shut right into another world war. Still, he did not allow himself to stray from the party line. Stalin must have had good reasons, some of his friends said; there was a conspiracy against the Soviet Union and against the French Communist party.

To justify its position, *L'Humanité*, the official voice of the party, condemned Paris and London for legitimizing the fascist Franco government. The newspaper was seized, and the party dissolved. Its leaders accused of sedition against France's national defense fled. Some were caught, imprisoned, and brought to trial.

Eugène was again in a quandary, as were many of his compatriots. They knew that war was approaching. "What will I do? What should we do?" he asked. He had recently tailored a new suit for Monsieur Chatelet; he trusted him and had come to see him.

"Do I hide, or do I fight?" he asked bluntly.

Eugène already knew the answer. He had only come to hear it spelled out.

"You and your family are legal residents, but in times such as these, when foreigners are regarded with suspicion, their safety is uncertain." Hiding, thought Monsier Chatelet, increased vulnerability.

"If and when you are found, you run the risk of being deported, or else sent to a detention camp or worse. If I were you, I'd enlist in the French army. Your family will be entitled to the rights and protection any soldier fighting for France deserves. Don't worry, Monsieur Eugène, we will defeat these barbarian Nazis."

He reported the conversation to Carmen. They were expecting their second child and hoped it would be a girl. What chances for a normal life would that child have under the present conditions? They had already decided to name her Liliane if it was a girl, a derivation of lily of the valley, the small and gracious flower friends give each other in spring for good luck.

And then all hell broke loose. Without a declaration of war, Hitler invaded Poland and overran it. General mobilization ensued simultaneously in France and in England. Like thousands of others, Eugène reported to the Commissariat of Police to enlist. He joined up as a first-

PART ONE—EUGÈNE & CARMEN
CHAPTER FIFTEEN

class soldier in the 21st infantry regiment. The rank sounded martial and manly, but he soon realized that a foot soldier's life was very trying. They marched for hours on end, and though he considered himself fit, he was exhausted at the end of each day.

For the French, the war began 3 September 1939, at five o'clock in the afternoon. Eugène left home two days later to undergo basic training that lasted until January. He returned home twice to visit and say goodbye to his family before joining his regiment.

Though sad to be leaving their wives and children, soldiers of all ranks were joyful and optimistic. They assumed the war would be short and that they would win it. The military encouraged these beliefs. They claimed that *La Ligne Maginot*, a powerful line of defense that stretched from Switzerland to the Ardennes in the north, and from the Alps to the Mediterranean in the south, would protect them.

Built between 1929 and 1940, postwar military strategists imagined it as a vast, ultramodern defensive system, a guarantee that the French nation as a whole would remain indestructible. But in reality the Maginot Line was only an early defense system against a German attack on France's eastern frontier. When the Germans invaded, the Maginot Line allowed the French army time to mobilize fully. But Hitler and his rapid all-terrain tanks simply bypassed it. After the swift defeat of France, the German invaders used Maginot and its intricate system of bunkers to continue the fight against the Allies.

Eugène's unit became prisoners of the Germans on 18 June 1940, in the lovely little city of Lure, near Beaufort, in the Haute-Savoie, itself not far away from the Maginot Line. They had seen no fighting and were stunned by their country's swift defeat.

The majestic Alps loomed high above their troubles. Everything was green and blooming in this glowing summer weather. They were defeated but for the time behaved like brothers sent to camp for a retreat or a special workshop. The respite was brief. Soon they were packed in trains bound for Austria, where they arrived dizzy with tiredness and hungry as wolves.

They were deposited in the prison camp Stalag 17 A near the town of Kaisersteinbruch. They expected no welcome party, of course, but were deeply disappointed by the skimpy meal they were finally served—a thin soup with a few pieces of turnip swimming in undocumented fat, accompanied by one slice of stale bread.

"The party is over, prisoners," barked the German officer in charge of the camp over his loudspeaker.

"Tomorrow most of you will be sent to neighboring farms to help out with whatever chores need to be done. The farmers require help, and they might pay you some small sum for your labor. How much is entirely up to them. You will work there as long as your help is required. Do not try to escape. The area is heavily patrolled; you will be shot on sight if you try. As for those of you who are Jews, step out now. *Schnell!* We have special barracks for you."

Eugène looked around him to see who would obey this order. Some men stepped out hesitantly. He did not. Not out of fear, but simply because he felt like an equal member of the human race, the same as all the other prisoners of war. He figured that unless the German in command made him drop his pants, he'd have no way to know if he, Eugène Grozinger, was a Christian or a Jew.

The next day he was sent to work on a farm five kilometers away

PART ONE—EUGÈNE & CARMEN
CHAPTER FIFTEEN

from the prisoner's camp. The farmer was a man in his sixties who had no words of kindness at his disposal. Eugène had to work from early morning until nightfall doing chores he was not well adapted to: clearing brush, cutting the trunks of fallen trees, carrying them back to the farm in a creaking wheelbarrow. His hands developed enormous calluses.

The farmer's family ate meat and drank wine in front of him. No offer forthcoming; they ignored him completely. They served him some crude porridge augmented with carrot peels. That was not a real meal, and his strength declined rapidly. At night, he was sent to retire in the barn on a pile of straw where he had a hard time falling asleep despite his fatigue. "This isn't good," he thought. "I have to do something fast to get out of this situation."

He knew that none of the Jewish prisoners ever left camp. That was because the Germans believed Jews knew nothing about agriculture or farming, that all they were interested in was making money by hook or by crook.

Before the war Eugène had visited the *Musée Carnavalet* in Paris with his wife and child. He was surprised when he stopped in front of a medieval ensign engraved with a Jewish star surrounded by bunches of grapes. Of course, there had been and would always be winemakers, farmers, and orchards cultivated by Jews. He knew firsthand the care his parents had given to their small plot of land; they had a relationship with the land, hoeing the ground and planting it with seeds to assure their sustenance.

"We Jews are not all bankers and landlords. We are not 'special' in that pejorative classification Nazis use against us," he declared.

When the German soldier came around to the farm to check the progress of his work, Eugène said he wanted to return to the Stalag.

"There's been an error," he informed the soldier. "I am not supposed to work here. I'm a Jew."

"You were under obligation to report that information right away, on the very first day of your arrival!" snarled the soldier.

"I did. It's probably some administrative error."

"We'll see about that. Get your things together while I speak to the farmer."

He hadn't made one pfennig for the miserable days of his hard labor, but he didn't complain. He hoped different opportunities would arise with his corrected status. He badly needed money for Carmen and the children and for his personal needs.

Most of the Jewish prisoners staying inside the camp did janitorial labor. Their chores included cleaning toilets, washing floors, disposing of smelly garbage, and carrying and washing the heavy pots, in which the so-called food was cooked.

Yet some of these prisoners possessed the kind of talent the Kommandant was looking for. Eugène was that kind. Questioned about his civilian trade, he proudly reported that he was a fine tailor.

"Prove it," ordered the German who conducted his interview.

"Yes, at your command, *Mein Herr*. Let me borrow a pair of good scissors, a needle, some thread, and something to repair," he said.

The German led him to a barrack where a few men were mending a stack of clothes.

"Easy. I can do that and more," promised Eugène.

He promptly repaired a large tear underneath the leg of a pair of

PART ONE—EUGÈNE & CARMEN
CHAPTER FIFTEEN

pants, and showed the results to the German.

"*Schon gut! It's O.K. Arbeit schnell. Hurry!* That sewing machine over there is yours."

"If you please, one more thing, Kommandant, my hands are swollen and callused. Let me rest a few days. When they get better, I'll make you a suit, a coat, whatever you want. Some solid, healthy food would also help me recover faster."

He knew he was pushing his luck, but he had always been an optimist. Something good has to happen once in a while.

The German coughed a couple times to give himself countenance. He growled something the tailor didn't understand, but for the next three days he was allowed to rest and fill his stomach as much as he could with potatoes lightly brushed with margarine. It was so much better, a thousand times better than the meager regular fare. He regained some strength and began working. With his needle and sartorial know-how, he could fix or create any garment, anytime, anywhere. There was plenty of work, and what with the obligatory maintenance and regular repair of clothes issued by the Geneva Conventions for the treatment of prisoners of war, they stayed very busy.

Eugène approached the French overseer, who in civilian life had been a salesman in a fancy men's shop on the Champs Élysées. That's why Jean was the manager of the wooden shack in which most of the Jewish prisoners worked. In good time, Eugène took him aside and told him he had a plan. They would organize most of the prisoners for the work of repairs and alterations; then those who excelled at their trade would work to produce extra clothing they could sell out of shop for profit. Eventually they would make money and share it among themselves. They spread these ideas through the barrack; everyone agreed to participate in the venture.

Eugène showed his comrades how to save cloth. It was a matter of cutting, both for economy's sake and for the opportunity to create. Like an architect or an engineer, he had a keen sense of space and volume, and with the remnants of cloth, depending on the amount saved, they manufactured coats, pants, vests, scarves, and even pajamas.

Jean, the former salesman, took charge of the underground business. He had a real flair for this type of work. He decided to give a vest to Otto, their German overseer.

This man was a plain, older soldier who missed his civilian job and worried about his family back home. The gift pleased him enormously. He looked at himself in the fragment of mirror hanging on the wall and found his image to his liking.

Jean asked if there was any way Otto could provide the prisoners with surplus textiles. Winter was coming and warmer clothing was needed for the entire Stalag.

Otto understood, and he tried his best. After a while he found some promising contacts and returned with good news. Together the prisoners began their black market venture. They made pants and overcoats for the POWs, and with the surplus material they styled skirts and jackets that Otto marketed to the German officers, who bought them as presents for their wives and friends back home. Otto paid the prisoners back with money, food, and cigarettes. Everyone in their barrack received welcome supplements to their diet, including vegetables and fruits and even on a blessed day some real coffee.

A friendly atmosphere prevailed among the tailors. They knew

PART ONE—EUGÈNE & CARMEN
CHAPTER FIFTEEN

what they were working for and cooperated eagerly. Lest one misunderstand, fulfilling the quotas of production for the Germans was their duty and priority. If noticed, their extra little business would be judged seditious. And not everyone was like Otto. They took care not to steal too many hours away from the German boot, only just enough to produce "their own cream and butter rewards."

Eugène bought an old suitcase and filled it with cigarettes, the favorite currency of POWs. It was an important asset for trading and bartering. This state of affairs lasted about a year. Then Otto was assigned to another Stalag, and overnight the bounty ended. Everyone was forced to tighten their belts, and once more their stomachs growled.

One day Eugène received a package from little Szego and almost cried. He thought it an audacious gesture for a man who himself was in hiding. Every once in a while Carmen also sent a package of food and photographs of the children.

His son, Fred, was almost six years old; the look on his face was painfully serious. He was war's child, innocent yet marked, already disillusioned about humankind. He must have felt abandoned by his father; perhaps he had even forgotten him. How could the young boy understand his father's long absence?

His daughter, Liliane, was still tiny, but growing quickly. He had only seen her in the photos he received. She too seemed a bit serious, perhaps because someone told her to look at "the little bird."

Carmen, with a child on each side, stood proud and graceful, beautiful as ever.

He proudly showed his photos to his best buddy, Marcel Greilsamaer. He too had a family to show to Eugène. They had the same concerns; as a result their friendship grew.

At first they waited for liberation with patience, then after two and three years with exasperation and then with resignation. They entered their fourth year as prisoners of war still together.

They all harbored the same hope. They were more than ready to go home, to see their families and reacquaint themselves with their wives and children, to resume their careers, to enjoy a free and peaceful life.

Soon after Otto's departure they were sent to a margarine production plant. They suddenly felt like mice trapped in a cheese factory. No one could prevent them from helping themselves. Diverting a small percentage of the output became a skill, and if, perchance, they found some potatoes, they had a feast.

Their designated cook was a Polish emigrant to France, Yitzhak by name. He was a skinny, nervous fellow who isolated himself twice a day to sway forward and backward while reciting his Hebrew prayers.

"Some other time, fellow, will you? I'm hungry," called Marcel impatiently.

Yitzhak's French was execrable; the other prisoners teased him mercilessly about it. Of course that increased his nervousness. He couldn't remember who wanted what or how they wanted it cooked. "Can't you speak French?" someone was always complaining.

The periods of slight betterment were few and far between. Toward the end of the war, when the Germans retreated and pushed them onward, the prisoners existed on starvation diets while marching for days on end. On one such day as night fell upon them, they were directed toward a large barn.

PART ONE—EUGÈNE & CARMEN
CHAPTER FIFTEEN

They were shoved inside and to their horror began stumbling, falling on each other. They discovered hundreds of bodies stacked in rows like sardines, one on top of another. Those emaciated victims were Russians POWs. Their skin had turned the color of parchment. In spite of the dreadful smell of decomposition the prisoners fell to the ground. Most were vomiting. Everybody was struggling, too exhausted to take another step, now oblivious of the nearby dead.

In that awful place, during that awful night, Eugène was unable to close his eyes; a putrid smell was penetrating his nostrils and invading his brain. He felt nauseated and dizzy, his heartbeat increased. Suddenly he heard Marcel moaning by his side in his sleep. The lament was eerie, and Eugène felt his fear increasing. He shook Marcel awake.

Marcel, an intellectual with a Ph.D. in history, the most unassuming person he had ever known, looked past him as if seeking an invisible exit. "Marcel, Marcel," pleaded Eugène. "Wake up! Wake up!" He finally opened his eyes and assessed the situation. He took a handkerchief out of his pocket and wiped Eugène's brow tenderly.

"Don't worry, my friend," he said. "They'll make us or some other poor bastards bury those corpses, if only to hide their crimes. All the same we are witnesses, we will testify on their day of judgment."

So many corpses! The Nazis were running out of time. Plenty of evidence would be left to hang their leaders, they hoped.

After the liberation, Marcel returned to Vichy to resume life with his family. Teaching high school kids, he told Eugène, was his salvation. It kept his mind busy and helped him chase the ghosts. He felt proud rearing the new generation. They swore to stay in touch, to see one another at least a couple times a year. Marcel wrote to tell his friend he was writing a book and had some questions to ask. He wanted to verify certain aspects of their detention. But the promise to keep in touch proved more difficult to fulfill than either one of them thought. When my father finally wrote Marcel back, it was his buddy's wife who answered. She gave him the bad news; his friend was dead. Run over by a car driven by a drunk driver.

I have two photographs of my father with Marcel, both small, black-and-white prints taken at the prison camp. One shows them in a group of their mates; my father is smoking a cigarette. He appears solemn, squinting a little in the light. In the second one, the two friends stand shoulder to shoulder not quite able to give the camera a full smile.

Chapter Sixteen

Eugène had joined his battalion to fight the enemy. He became a prisoner of war barely six months after he left. France was defeated, and it had a new government that did not like his kind and imposed dire restrictions on them.

Unlike Eugène who enlisted to serve in the war, his older brother Elias chose to go into hiding. He left Paris alone to find a safe place for his family in the town of Périgueux in what was still unoccupied France. There on the outskirts of town he found a rental house and made ready to welcome his wife, his wife's elderly mother, and his daughter, Eveline. Elias had arranged for a *passeur*, a person who knew the area well and who sold his services to people seeking to leave the more dangerous German occupied zone for the unoccupied, somewhat safer part of France called "the free zone."

One day during the time when Carmen was agonizing about whether or not to send her children to the South in care of the Association of Prisoners of War, someone knocked hurriedly at the door of her apartment in the rue des Tournelles. She was not anxious to open the door and took her time answering. Finally, she heard a small voice.

"Open up; it's me, Eveline!"

She welcomed her niece in. She hadn't seen her in a long time. Eveline lived in Clermont-Ferrand with her family. "What are you doing alone in Paris?" she asked. "Where is your mother? Has something happened?"

"I am here all by myself, Tante Carmen," Eveline explained.

"My mother, my grandmother, and I were about to cross into unoccupied France to join my father. But the French police arrested us. Someone must have warned them. They were waiting for us. We had no time to run away. We begged them to let us go. They replied, 'Orders,' and drove us in their car to Paris. Once there, I was taken away from my mother and my grandmother. I was kicking and screaming, but no one seemed to care. I didn't even get to take a last look at them, but I did hear my mother's voice as she was being taken away. She said, 'I love you, *mamala*. Be brave my darling.' Then I was taken someplace in a van and delivered to a big six-floor building full of Jewish children of all ages."

She stopped and asked for a glass of water. Carmen fetched it; the girl drank it in one gulp.

"My poor darling," said Carmen, drying the tears on her own face, but trying hard to hold them in. "How did you manage to escape?" she asked.

"I spent four days in that building. I knew that sooner or later we would be taken to some horrible place where we would probably die. Also, I heard a rumor that we were about to be transported to an internment camp in the suburbs of Paris. I wasn't waiting to find out. I began observing the sentinel keeping watch in the street right in front of the building, watching when the shift changed. Here was my chance, and with luck, my way to freedom."

"I didn't sleep the night I planned my escape. It was still dark at

PART ONE—EUGÈNE & CARMEN
CHAPTER SIXTEEN

five in the morning; I was ready to go. I'd rehearsed the whole thing with imaginary wings during the night. Nothing was going to stop me. No one woke up. I looked through the window. It was cold and foggy outside. Better for me to hide! I grabbed the sheets I had twisted into a rope. It was too short, but I did not care. I jumped about two meters to the ground and landed on my knees. They're scraped. I bled some. But I'm fine, I don't feel any pain."

"Oh, you brave girl, let me see," Carmen said.

"Don't bother, it will heal. Let me go, Aunty, I'm in a hurry."

"Go where?" she asked the child.

"To join my father. I know how to get there. I studied the map Papa had sent us several times, and again on the day we left, before meeting the *passeur*. I'm going to take the train. I'll walk the rest of the way. It's just over a hill, a kilometer past the train station. I'm not carrying a suitcase, but if I need anything, I have some money sewn in the hem of my coat. I know what to do; I'll walk in plain sight, like any normal child. No one will pay attention to me, trust me. I just came by so you'd know what happened to Mama and Grandmama. I must go now."

"Wait, I'll make you a sandwich. Here take some water with you. Send me a postcard to let me know you arrived safely."

Eveline left. Carmen's eyes filled with tears. Little Eveline, such a tough girl forced to make important and hasty decisions, who had not shed a tear for her mother and her grandmother. Eveline was changed, her feelings hardened. She was already a survivor.

Her postcard arrived a week later. It said, "Hello and kisses from Elias and Eveline."

Eveline remained hidden with her father until the end of the war. She turned sixteen and shortly after that moved back to Paris to resume her studies. Her father rented an apartment where she lived by herself. She became part of the postwar jazz scene. Her English was good, and after she graduated, Eveline took a translator's job with NATO. She became an Existentialist, then a Marxist, and an anti-Zionist after marrying a like-minded American soldier. They moved to New York with Dominique, a daughter from her former marriage to a jazz musician.

There is a photo of Eveline's mother, taken before her disappearance, in Carmen's album. She was a big-boned woman with a huge smile, holding baby Liliane in her arms.

Her name was Rivka Grozinger. Eveline resembles her. She may have been a cheerful woman; she may have been dull. Eugène remembered that she talked constantly and was loud. Like any of us, she was endowed with the right to life, liberty and the pursuit of happiness. She was robbed of all that in a single day, arrested and later marched into a gas chamber from which her body was removed minutes later to be shoved in a crematorium, there transformed into ashes. This state of affairs repeated with the next individual, in the same way, through torture, starvation, hanging, disease incurred from proximity and lack of hygiene, six million times and more, counting Romish and non-Jews of many creeds and nationalities.

Chapter Seventeen

Liliane and the war arrived together. She was born on a frigid and rainy day in November 1940. Her mother looked at her with awe. Her hands, fingers, legs, feet, and toes were perfect. She is beautiful, Carmen cried. She couldn't wait to take her home and show her to Fred, that resourceful boy who walked all the way to the wholesale market of Les Halles to pick up anything that was bruised and rejected or given to him by the sellers: a cabbage, some carrots, squash and leeks, anything else that might help them survive during that time of deprivation. Their savings were dwindling; without the small pension received from the Association of Prisoners of War, and Fred's finds, they would have starved.

Not long after the Germans occupied Paris, special measures were taken against Jews. They had to register. Fred and she were obliged to sew big yellow Jewish stars on their coats. These served as signs of opprobrium, as marks of shame. They couldn't do this, they couldn't do that, could not sit on a bench in the park, could not go to the movies. Jewish doctors, nurses, lawyers, architects, and politicians were forbidden from exercising their professions. Their property was confiscated and sold. They no longer had a way to make a living. The list of humiliations they endured was unending. Some establishments even posted signs announcing they no longer received dogs or people of the Hebrew persuasion, in that order. It was no use asking why their lives were being destroyed. She could break her teeth on the reasons, which were imperviously simple. They were ostracized because they were who they were.

Carmen suffered under these conditions and worried about Fred. Her son didn't ask any questions, but outside their home and in the streets his small face tightened, his teeth were clenched. Nothing could make him laugh again. Like everybody else in the neighborhood they heard about the *rafle du Vélodrome d'Hiver*, the French police operation that took place in July 1942, during which nearly eighteen thousand Parisian Jews and their children were rounded up and sent to the large Vélodrome d'Hiver stadium. After several days without food, water, or sanitation they were packed off to Drancy and eventually Auschwitz.

Carmen had studied the history of Jews and read many books about them on her own. They were human beings; they were an ancient people who had brought monotheism to the world and witnessed the birth of two other main religions whose roots dug deep into their own. After the Crusades and burnings of Jews; after the Spanish and Portuguese Inquisitions with their grotesque apparatus of justice against Jews who had fearfully converted, because they were tired of living like pariahs; after the pogroms in Russia, in Poland, all over Eastern Europe; after resettlement and forced emigration from France, England, and the city states of Italy; after the accusations against them during the great plagues that resulted in their slaughter, Jews dared to survive. In the eyes of their enemies, they deserved to suffer cruel deaths and total destruction of their families. It was

PART ONE—EUGÈNE & CARMEN
CHAPTER SEVENTEEN

impossible to combat such flawed logic. Murder and robbery satisfied both racists profiteers, as well as petty criminals.

Anti-Jewish propaganda abounded in Paris. Posters and movies clamored loudly and reached vast audiences. One film in particular was subtly titled *The Jew Süss*. It was a virulent indictment against the Jewish people, and was popular with the public. Carmen was curious to see it, and one day asked a friend to keep the baby while Fred was at school. She removed her Jewish star and snuck into the Bastille Cinema. The story, the marquee announced, was based on true events.

The Jew Süss turned out to be what she feared: propaganda that encouraged utter contempt and hatred of the Jews. The action takes place in 1754. Jews are second-class citizens confined to certain areas, barred from settling in certain cities. Among the population of a certain city-state lives one wealthy Jew. He is Josef Süss Oppenheimer, well-educated and versed in business practice.

His orthodox minions wear yarmulkes and bear straggly beards and curly locks. Of course they yearn for emancipation and dream to obtain permission to settle beyond their ghettoized life. They wish to have the same rights enjoyed by the citizens of the area, and they look up to Süss to procure those wishes. Their wealthy and resourceful colleague is the intimate of a gentile, a duke who appreciates Süss's business acumen. Soon enough, complaints arise. The tradesmen and the members of the City Council denounce Süss's practices. They claim angrily that he is filling the duke's pockets while the tactics he uses to perform these results are ruining everyone else.

At long last, he is arrested and charged with many crimes, some specific, others imagined, the most significant of which being his alleged rape of the beautiful wife of a jealous city counselor. The frightened woman commits suicide; Süss is charged with murder and sentenced to death. "Jewish blood cannot be allowed to contaminate Christian blood, not now, not in any future," the city counselors advise the town assembly.

Süss is put into a cage and hanged before day's end. His followers have taken flight; order is restored. The duty of true Aryans is clear-cut: eliminate the pestilential Jews for all generations to come.

The word "contaminate" made Carmen shudder. There was applause in the audience. She could hardly believe the universal reaction. She ran out of the theater before the lights came back on. She was scared because she now understood that most people believed what they saw. She was alone, insignificant, scared for her children and for the many other helpless people already engulfed in this powerful wave of hate.

In the face of all this, she endeavored to give Fred and Liliane whatever she could. She shepherded them and attempted to brighten their childhood as much as possible during this terrible period. It was difficult to smile and to look happy, but she tried. There were clothes and shoes to be bought, and no matter the state of her finances, she saw it as her duty to her boy and her baby girl to record the progress of their growth. Whenever she had a little surplus cash, she took them to the photographer's shop dressed in their best, hair carefully combed, wearing their whites gloves and their shiny shoes. Carmen sent copies of the photographs to Eugène and to her family in the United States, and, for safety's sake, entrusted a set with her good neighbors René and Mathilde Raby.

PART ONE—EUGÈNE & CARMEN
CHAPTER SEVENTEEN

This couple was already in their late forties and had long wished for a child. Mathilde was especially eager to keep Liliane and take care of her. When things became really difficult, as Jews were being arrested in the middle of the night and transported to French internment camps for triage and later deportation to concentration camps, Mathilde made an offer. She spoke about the dangers the children and Carmen faced. She said she worried about them. She wanted to help and offered to adopt Liliane. Carmen was shocked, but she told Mathilde she would think about it. She fell into a state of confusion, and confided in her few friends, asking them what to do. Finally, she knocked on Mathilde's door and told her she couldn't give her child up. Thanking her for her concern and generosity, she explained that against all odds, their family would be reunited.

Mathilde was disappointed, but fortunately her feelings for them did not change. Even though Carmen had good friends, whether Jewish or not who did what they could to help by providing her with black market food and showing her other kindnesses, her fears continued to increase. One day a social worker affiliated with the Association of Prisoners of War came to see her.

"I have good news for you," she said. "The APW can send your children to the south of France for the summer. It will do them good to breathe some fresh air and eat some good wholesome food."

"I'd rather keep them with me," Carmen told her. "I would feel lost without them."

"I understand how you feel, but I can guarantee you they will be safe there, much more than if they stayed in Paris," she added. "Just think about it."

Again she sought counsel from friends, from Dinah who had twin girls and worried about them. Her own status was less secure as she was not the wife of a POW. She said it seemed a good thing: Carmen was lucky to be protected by the APW. Furthermore, the Prisoners' organization was paying the host families for shelter, food, and care.

"It's not like you're giving your children away. You'll know the name and address of the host family and will be able to communicate with them."

When the social worker returned a few days later, Carmen told her she was ready to enroll her Fred, who was then seven years old.

"What about your little girl?" she asked.

"Liliane is only two and a half. She still wears diapers at night. She is too young to be separated from her mother. I think she'll be better off staying with me."

"Wait, let me come back next week. We usually don't take children that young, but Liliane has an older brother who can take care of her during the trip so we may be able to make an exception. I want the best for you and your children. Please take time to think things through. We are all prisoners in our country, but you and your children are more vulnerable than most. I urge you to reconsider."

Finally, Carmen let both of her children go, thinking it was just for the summer.

Chapter Eighteen

Do you know what it means to be taken away from your home? How could Carmen ever forget it?

Someone was banging on her door. Her eyes opened wide. She looked at the clock. Five in the morning. Her heartbeat surged, revving up like a frantic engine.

She knew immediately who was behind the door. For weeks rumors had it that Jewish people were being taken out of their homes during the early morning hours. She had a friend who never spent the night twice in the same place. That didn't help; the concierge alerted the police, who came to arrest him.

"Stop banging on the door. I'm dressing," she shouted.

She grabbed her papers and opened the door. The man standing in front of her was a tall policeman with an unsmiling face.

"What do you want?" she said, trying not to look afraid.

"Hurry up. Pack a suitcase and come with me," he answered.

She demanded an explanation and protested vehemently. She told the policeman that she had committed no crime, that she was the wife of a prisoner of war, a fighter for France who had volunteered, whose family was protected from harm and harassment by the Geneva Conventions.

"Just obeying orders. Get going," he replied in a calm voice.

She would always remember how clean-shaven he was, with skin as smooth as a peach, and how warm and cozy he must have felt with the heavy turtleneck he wore under his thick leather jacket.

She got a small suitcase and began packing like an automaton. How can one pack her life in a single suitcase, she wondered? Her mind was numb, her eyes veiled with tears. At last her hands took over.

Cold. It would always be cold from now on, she thought. She grabbed her warmest sweater, her warmest nightgown, socks and skirt, her bedroom shoes, clean underwear, a raincoat; then turned to the bookshelf and pulled a book out of it at random.

"Never go out without a book," she remembered her brother Maurice saying when she was young. "You never know when something unexpected will happen and leave you with nothing to do."

She also wanted her family pictures but refrained. No hint of who her children were and what they looked like must fall into the hands of their persecutors.

"When will I be back?" she asked the policeman.

"I don't know, Madame. Perhaps they'll tell you when you arrive at your destination."

"Where are you taking me? I have the right to know," she insisted.

"You'll know when you get there," he repeated without looking at her.

She locked her front door and thought how illusory this gesture of ordinary protection against unwanted visitors was. They could always come in, break the door, and drag her out.

Out on the landing, she made a lot of noise, banged her bag against the walls and began sobbing. She wanted Mathilde and René Raby to hear her and be witnesses. She knew Mathilde slept lightly, and she was not disappointed.

PART ONE—EUGÈNE & CARMEN
CHAPTER EIGHTEEN

Within seconds, her neighbor's frizzy hair and half her face appeared in the corner of her front door. Carmen was following the dutiful *agent de police*, but not too fast. She decided to trip and fell against the timer that turned the electricity in the hallway on and off, plunging everyone in temporary darkness, just like she hoped. This gave her the opportunity to slide her key under Mathilde's doormat.

She got up again and shouted, "They're taking me away! Write Eugène! Tell him what happened."

The policeman flicked his lighter on to find the switch in the darkness. "Stop shouting," he said harshly. "We're not here to alert the entire neighborhood."

She picked up her suitcase and turned her head toward Mathilde's door. Her neighbor's anxious face no longer appeared, but she trusted her neighbors would keep an eye on her apartment.

Three buses were parked in front of the building, ordinary white and green buses, the kind you wait for in the street in front of a post bearing the bus number and its destination, the kind that has a platform at the end of the bus on which you can stand to see the sights of Paris freely.

Inside each bus waited women and their half-awake children. Some of them were frightened. They murmured, "Mommy, where are we going? It's dark, and I'm cold. I want my bed." Their mothers attempted to quiet and soothe them.

Carmen looked around. The light of the day had not yet broken through, and it was difficult to see faces in the dark. She strained her eyes and recognized some of the women and children in the seats in front of and behind her. They had gone to some of the meetings she had also attended. All of them were wives and children of prisoners of war.

THE BONES OF TIME

The buses converged in front of the Gare d'Austerlitz. There the passengers were asked to embark onto a larger vehicle that immediately made its way to the gray, foggy suburbs outside of the city they loved.

The families of prisoners of war extracted from their homes by night during November 1943 spent the next five months in Drancy, a small city northeast of Paris, which would later become famous for the horrors that occurred there. The detention camp consisted of several unfinished buildings, four to five floors in height, arranged in a U-shape, beyond which several guard towers had been added.

The raw cement buildings that became home to the new detainees had been a 1930s avant-garde project that offered an array of gardens and city living. The project, however, had fallen on hard times. Unfinished and abandoned, *La Muette*, as it was to have been named, was now the Drancy detention camp.

The tired and anguished women and children who entered these facilities were marched through narrow hallways that led into a small room. There, their names and identities were duly verified. When that task was completed, they were invited to deposit money and valuables in the hands of an *agent de police* sitting at another table. The sum they took from Carmen's wallet amounted to three hundred and thirty-five francs. The transaction was inventoried in a professional manner, as if the internees were willing participants carrying out ordinary financial affairs. They were even given receipts bearing an account number.

"Perhaps," whispered one of the women hopefully, "this careful accounting means they'll soon send us home."

Then came the SS men. They carried files that helped them conduct interrogations. Carmen's name was called.

PART ONE—EUGÈNE & CARMEN
CHAPTER EIGHTEEN

"Carmen Grozinger?" asked her interrogator without raising his head. "Yes," she nodded. She glanced at him. His demeanor, the way he held his head screamed self-satisfaction, order, and authority.

"Here is your dossier. You are a Jew, married to a Jew; you have two children. Where are they?" asked the SS man in a calm, unthreatening voice. "Relax, you can tell me. We only wish to reunite you with your family."

"I don't know," Carmen replied in her native German.

"You speak good German. So we understand one another. How is it you don't know where your children are? Such young children! They didn't just disappear, did they?"

She felt tired and hungry but resolved. He could kill her; she would never reveal her children's whereabouts. "Yesterday," she began confidently, "I was waiting in line at the grocery store to get some milk. Everyone was pushing and shoving. My friend said she'd take my children to her home if I shared the milk with her later. We often help each other that way. It was getting late, and I didn't want to go out after curfew. I knew it was fine with my friend, that if I was too late my kids could spend the night at her place. I was going to go collect them today, but the police picked me up."

"Stop it, stop immediately," he suddenly shouted. "You don't really think I believe your stupid story, do you? Don't waste my time! I'll ask you once more, and mind your answer! It will make the difference between your staying in Drancy for a while, or being shipped to Auschwitz immediately."

His demeanor had changed. He was livid; he slammed his hands on his desk, got up, and lunged toward her. She thought he was about to hit her. Instead, he pushed her hard into a chair. Carmen looked down at his boots. They shone like mirrors, twice reflecting her diminishing face.

"Once more, your children are Fred, a boy seven years old, and a girl, Liliane, two years old. Where are they?"

His violent intonation disturbed the air between them, creating volutes, miniature storms crashing upon her visage. Did he think she was dumb or scared enough to give him any information about her precious children?

Suddenly a telephone rang.

"Captain Fuhrman," a subaltern called, "you're wanted on the telephone."

"All right," Fuhrman hissed, "Don't move, I'm coming back for you. We'll soon resume our little talk."

She waited on the chair. A hundred thoughts were rushing through her mind. She was thinking about the social worker who had begged her to send her children away, about Eugène who thought his family safe, about her parents who were beginning a new life in the United States, and about Ferry, the younger brother she might never see again.

The other women and their children were being processed. The French police took over. She was includud along with the group. Somehow, Captain Fuhrman did not come after her. Perhaps he had been wanted for a more important job. He could go to hell where he belonged as far as she was concerned. At any rate, she did not lose time pondering his whereabouts or this change in her fate. Later, through the grapevine, she heard about another mother, also interrogated by an SS officer, who like herself had refused to reveal her

PART ONE—EUGÈNE & CARMEN
CHAPTER EIGHTEEN

children's whereabouts. The poor woman had been severely beaten and sent on a train directly to Auschwitz.

Meanwhile, their entire group of women and children were moved to what would become their living quarters. The inside of the building had no doors, no walls, no windows, and no running water. The cement staircases taking them to the next floor had no handrails. They led to the naked platforms that became home to the hundreds of women and children parked there.

For months they lived and slept on pallets, washed their bodies and clothing in a courtyard where a long tub equipped with a few water faucets had been installed. The water was cold, their privacy restricted to the barest minimum.

Another area contained the toilets, mere holes above ground that smelled awful, where one could go only under the surveillance of a guard beneath the glare of the ubiquitous floodlights housed in the surrounding towers.

Once they had taken care of their daily hygiene, there was absolutely nothing for the adults and their children to do. An immense feeling of boredom and despair descended over the group, but within a few days some of the inmates organized themselves to better care for the children. Friendships between the women began to form. The older children were called upon to teach the younger ones. Surprisingly, one woman, then another, then a third revealed herself to be a born storyteller. Together they managed to entertain the youngsters for an hour or so. Anyone who had brought along a precious book passed it on to the others.

Carmen's own dog-eared book made the round of the adults. It was a detective story in which the perpetrators of evil were caught in their underground tunnels of crime. This book momentarily quenched the thirst for justice of those who read it fitfully in the barebones building of the Drancy detention camp, whose unfortunate inhabitants were always cold and always hungry.

Sometimes a package arrived destined for someone lucky enough to be remembered by friends. Mathilde and René had not forgotten Carmen. They sent what they could, some coffee, a pot of jelly, a loaf of bread, even hard salami that could last for days without spoiling. She shared these treasures with a few others, and then they in turn shared food someone else had sent them.

At times the prisoners were distracted and frightened by what happened around them. Across the barbed wire area separating the women from other groups, people's names were called. When this occurred, the individuals who stood up did not protest. They went fast, without making noise. They were shoved into trains or vans taking them to some unknown destination. When asked, the mothers would tell their children that the people were en route to a mythical place called "Pitchipoi," a nonsense word their sons and daughters believed meant 'castle.'

They knew that all the families of prisoners of war would eventually be selected for a nebulous destination no one wanted to mention. Carmen's turn arrived soon enough. She was made to gather her few belongings along with the others called forward. The collective fear made her nervous and withdrawn. The children turned paler, quieter.

Drancy was bad enough. How much worse could their circumstances become? To what new hell were they being sent?

Chapter Nineteen

After a voyage of two days in third-class train cars, with little water or food and ghastly sanitary conditions, convoy number 80, grouping one hundred and seventy-seven women and seventy-seven children, fifteen of whom traveled without parents, arrived in Bergen-Belsen on the night of 2 May 1944, tired and traumatized. They were brutally pushed out of the wagons with shouts and blows that fell on those who did not move fast enough.

The grayish light of dawn appeared shortly thereafter. Once more the women and children were told to run through muddy ground in order to be accounted for, a procedure that seemed very important to the Nazis, who counted and recounted people anytime they wished, in any sort of weather, even after the people became walking corpses, even after they were dead.

The camp consisted of groups of barracks, each separated by barbed wire, enclosing nineteen thousand people of different ethnicities and languages.

Carmen's group was known as *Camp de l'étoile* because of the yellow star still affixed to the clothes they had brought from Drancy. These garments soon deteriorated. In the end, they were left wearing whatever they could scrounge from the clothes the dead left behind.

Life in Bergen-Belsen was a horribly obscene *Commedia dell'arte*. The props were mean and meager: planks for beds, crowded barracks, barbed wires, a crematorium. The protagonists included those who wore shiny boots, carried guns and whips, and delivered pain and insults to their prisoners. The prisoners for their part wore rags and newspapers in their shoes, if they still had some, to combat the exceptionally harsh conditions.

Those who had the energy and the willpower washed their wasted bodies with water trickling from a half-frozen faucet, while the well-fed soldiers watching them laughed out loud, pointing out the grotesque figures they had become.

Carmen's hope to regain her freedom receded rapidly, though she took pains to continue to wash her body. Ceasing to do so would be a death warrant; vermin and malnutrition combined to take a soul in very little time.

Carmen suffered pain, hunger, and diseases like the other inmates. Some of them endeared themselves to their guards in order to survive and became torturers themselves, betraying their own sense of human kindness and adding shame to their misery.

This was the kind of life my mother shared and barely endured. At first, some of the women managed to help each other cooperatively, to take care of one another, especially the children: this in conditions that did not nurture life and worsened day after day. There were so many ways to die: cold, starvation, exhaustion, typhus, and dysentery. They were sent to do hard labor, tortured, beaten to death, or shot. They could try to steal food, or attempt escape, only to run into the barbed wire.

PART ONE—EUGÈNE & CARMEN
CHAPTER NINETEEN

Who were the lucky ones? Those who died quickly, or those who survived to wake up with nightmares for the rest of their lives?

What else can be said about Bergen-Belsen? The air above and around it was fouled by the smell of burned flesh. There were dead and dying people everywhere. Some might be your friends, but you were too weak to pity or mourn them. The fleas in your clothes, on your flesh, on your head were relentless, made you sick, made you want to die. You could be robbed, shot by a sadistic guard, tortured, starved to death, or used for experiments.

At times, Carmen wanted to die to stop this wasted, meaningless living. At other times, she wanted to survive to see the day that would certainly come, when the rest of the world came to free them from these demons. If and when that happened, she hoped there would still be a part of her that remembered how to love her children, her husband, and her friends.

Chapter Twenty

In spite of the friendships they made and the lively conversation they shared, the prisoners of Stalag 17 were plagued by depression. They labored under harsh conditions, and they were losing hope. This war stretched behind them like a long, threadbare rug. They were tired of seeing it. They wanted to burn it; they wished to go home.

The food situation had progressively deteriorated over the last two years. It was scarce and of poor quality; sometimes there was no food at all. Hunger was the wolf continually chasing them. The days of the margarine plant bounty now seemed far behind them. They dreamt about *pot au feu*, the beef soup of leeks, potatoes, and carrots, accompanied by mustard that could settle the heart and free the mind. When they were together they talked about recipes, a meager substitute for real food that was absent in their lives.

At first, Eugène depended on Carmen to send him eagerly awaited packages. When they arrived, he felt a sense of exultation, a mixture of warmth and love that lasted a few days. He never failed to share the contents of his package with friends, who in turn shared with him what they received from their own families. The additional calories helped them survive the worst of cold weather and forced labor. Because of further restrictions, he, like others, learned to be frugal. Additional hardships after the Liberation convinced him to remain spartan for the course of his life.

Toward the end of December 1943, he received a letter from the Rabys. Carmen had been arrested and taken to Drancy detention camp. His tears flowed uncontrollably. He had failed to protect his wife; the French police had arrested her. The very country he had chosen to fight for was betraying him. Didn't the Geneva Conventions contain provisions for the care and treatment of prisoners of war and their families?

Eugène remembered Mr. Chatelet's reassurances in those days before the war became a certainty. Old man Pétain, this traitor, this collaborator, had sold out to the Nazis. The French police were their heartless lackeys. For them, an order was just an order to be carried out without thought or feeling. Where was their conscience, their heart?

No, an order could not just be an order when given by evil people to perpetrate evil. And who in their right mind would agree to follow vicious orders, to pull innocent people out of their homes in the middle of the night to take them to prison? What kind of government was the Vichy government that persecuted people on grounds of their racial appurtenance and sold them to the German apparatus of degradation and death?

He was crazy with resentment—his buddies tried to comfort him. He was not the only one who suffered, they pointed out. Others faced the same situation and worse; their children, many of them no older than five, had been caught in the same net. At least Eugène knew his son and daughter to be safe somewhere in the south of France.

He racked his brains. What could he do for his wife at this point

PART ONE—EUGÈNE & CARMEN
CHAPTER TWENTY

outside of hoping that her status as a "wife of prisoner of war" protected her from further persecution?

The Rabys sent him the detention camp's address and the number of the building in which Carmen was imprisoned. He hastened to send her a letter. He wasn't able to say the things he held in his heart. The Germans censored all communications. The small size of the official postcard the authorities provided further restricted what could be said. Eugène managed to hide the word "Espoir [hope]" in a sentence. He exchanged the cigarettes he had accumulated in the early days when he run the prisoners of war tailor's shop with profit. It was his turn to supply Carmen with packages. He sent money to Mathilde and René to buy some nonperishable food and some toiletries and wrote:

My darling Carmen,

    It's been a month since I received any news from you. I am sad, so sad about your being in Drancy. Good news about the children who are in good health. I got letters from Dora and Raymonde Levieux; also received a package from Szego. I'm waiting to hear from you. A thousand kisses to you, my darling.

                                              Love, Eugène

Chapter Twenty-One

Eugène was liberated on 20 November 1944 and repatriated a week later. When he returned to his apartment after four years of detention, the only thing he found inside was a bare light bulb hanging from a cord where the fixture had been. Everything Carmen and he had ever owned had disappeared. The emptiness of the place seeped into his body, lonely and cold.

He knocked at the Rabys' door. They welcomed him like a lost brother and told him about what happened the horrible night Carmen had been ordered out of their home at dawn, confused and terrified.

"We were awakened by her cries. We didn't realize what was going on and opened our door just a crack. Through it we heard and saw the police urging her to hurry," said Mathilde.

"It was the saddest thing," she continued, "to think that our own government arranged her arrest. It made me ashamed to be French. Our brave policemen! Just lackeys collaborating with those brutal invaders. We waved to Carmen from behind our windows; she may not have seen us but I am sure she knew we were witnesses."

They sent her packages when she was held at Drancy, and even managed to include a note saying they had tried to come see her there, but were denied entrance by camp authorities. Eugène told them that he was sure their care sustained her morale and helped her survive during the nearly five months she spent in Drancy, before she was dispatched to Bergen-Belsen.

René Raby suddenly told him, "Listen, *mon ami*, I have a surprise for you." He led Eugène into the adjoining room and asked him to uncover what seemed to be a very large object. There, before his eyes, stood his sewing machine.

"I went into your apartment immediately after they took Carmen," René proudly reported. "I knew I had to act fast to save it. It was darned heavy—I had to call Mathilde to help me."

"The next day some people came and took everything out of your apartment. I asked one guy why they were taking the belongings of a soldier who was fighting for France. He told me to mind my business. All the same, having retrieved your sewing machine felt good, like a victory for me, you, and your family."

René took three glasses out of his cupboard and filled them with cognac. They drank to what they most hoped for: survival for his Carmen and a speedy family reunification with their children. Eugène and Carmen remained friends with the Rabys until they died of old age.

Eugène left Paris for the south of France the next day. Thanks to the Association of Prisoners of War he knew exactly where his children were. He took the train at Gare d'Austerlitz and arrived six hours later in Labouheyre, a small city still about fifteen kilometers away from Sabres. It was an unusually warm day for the season. He felt the sun on his shoulders. He was still wearing his soldier's suit of clothes and the new heavy regulation boots issued to him upon his return from captivity. The train station was empty. The few people who had arrived in Labouheyre departed with their family or friends. He was alone on an empty platform.

PART ONE—EUGÈNE & CARMEN
CHAPTER TWENTY-ONE

He went out and looked around. On the sun-baked plaza, a café was open. In front of it, seated at a table, a man with a large face wearing a beret was sipping a drink.

"Hello," Eugène said, "Pardon me, could you tell me how I can get to Sabres?" The man put his glass down and considered the soldier in front of him. "You're not from around here, are you?" he asked with the distinctive accent of the region.

"No, I'm not. I come from Paris. Could you please tell me if there is a bus to travel from here to Sabres?"

"One every two days, son. You've just missed it."

He was tired and hungry and suddenly felt dizzy.

"Ho, ho," said the man, pulling a chair beside his own. "Sit down, soldier."

He called to someone inside. "*Hortense, une menthe à l'eau!* Nothing better to refresh you."

Eugène sat down and drank. "I have got to get to Sabres today," he insisted.

"You know somebody there?"

"I'm looking for a Monsieur Dublanc."

"That must be Raymond Dublanc. I know him; he's been the mayor of Sabres during this infernal war. What kind of business do you have with him, may I ask?"

"I'm coming to get my children. This good man and his family gave them a home during my absence. I'm anxious to see my son, and my little girl whose acquaintance I have yet to make."

"Have a bite to eat and tell me your story, why don't you?" the man said.

"No thanks, I ate when I left Paris."

"Nonsense! That was long ago. What would you say to a freshly caught trout in black butter served with morels? Don't worry, the bill's on me."

"I'm much obliged, Monsieur."

"Don't mention it. You've been a prisoner of war, haven't you?"

"Yes, for four long, wearisome years. During that time the French police arrested my wife. They took her to Drancy, and from there to Bergen-Belsen. I don't even know if she is alive. I'm going to pick up my boy, and I only hope he recognizes me. He was seven when I left."

"And the little girl?"

"She is much younger. I've never seen her. She doesn't know what her father looks like. I was already a prisoner when she was born. I don't think I can take care of her. Perhaps she can stay in Sabres a little longer."

The man's eyes were filling with tears; he could not contain his emotion.

"*Mon petit gars*, my boy. How terrible it is to tear a family apart like that. Poor France! What have we done? Here, eat, have a glass of wine. Relax a bit. Let's drink a toast to you, and to your wife. May she soon return in good health, and one more toast. To your children's safe future, to their happiness!"

The man pulled a large handkerchief out of his pocket and began sobbing. It was a long time since anyone had cried on Eugène's behalf. He had indeed endured much, more than a person may expect in a lifetime. But the man's unexpected reaction filled him with renewed apprehension; how would he manage two chidren without Carmen?

PART ONE—EUGÈNE & CARMEN
CHAPTER TWENTY-ONE

"Don't worry," continued the man, still crying. "Things will get better. They have to. Let's have our meal and our coffee. Afterward I'll drive you to Raymond Dublanc's myself."

The wine had gone to Eugène's head. He fell asleep during the ride. When he awoke he was riding through the middle of a pine forest blanketed with tall ferns. The air was fresh; everything was strikingly beautiful and peaceful. The car emerged from the forest and stopped. Eugène parted from his driver with many expressions of thanks and shakings of hands.

He found himself standing in front of an imposing house. On the portal by the gate he read *La Capéranie*. A house with a name! He rang the bell and waited for someone to greet him.

A grandmother opened the door. She was very old, dressed in black from head to toe, coiffed with a chignon on the back of her head, perhaps in her late eighties. Eugène took his kepi off and explained the purpose of his visit. She welcomed him in, made him sit down in a comfortable room, and offered refreshments.

"We were expecting you. We didn't know exactly when, but here you are. I am happy to meet you," she said. "The rest of the family will be in shortly, though I don't know when my son-in-law will be home. You'll want to talk with him, I presume. Tell me though, you won't take Liliane back with you immediately, will you?"

She looked at him beseechingly, like a penitent waiting for a reprieve.

"Now that you mention it, I wouldn't quite know what to do with her," he replied. "I'd probably have to place her in a temporary orphanage, same as I have to do with her brother Fred. I have nothing left in the apartment, no bed, and no furniture of any kind. The looters even took the light bulbs. It's going to take some time before I can get back on my feet."

A smile of relief appeared on the old lady's face. She patted his shoulder with a smile. "Don't worry, you can leave Liliane with us. We love her; we'll take good care of her."

He introduced himself to Madame Dublanc and her daughters, Paulette and Hélène, young women barely in their twenties. They were forthcoming enough, though he felt some reserve on their part. Perhaps they resented this foreigner who was coming to claim the little girl they all seemed to love like a daughter.

"Tell you what," Paulette suggested, "It's about two o'clock. I know you're anxious to meet Fred and Liliane. Why don't you go pick them up at school? I'll drop you off. I've talked to the teacher—she knows all about it. Just knock at the door; she'll let you in. Then you and Liliane can walk back to *La Capéranie*. It will give you an opportunity to get acquainted. The teacher will show you the way. Fred will come later—we have invited him for supper."

Carmen had sent photographs of the children during his captivity, but of course that had ended when she was arrested. Eugène wondered if he'd recognize them. Reentering their lives seemed a challenging proposition.

He knocked to get inside the girls' school. The teacher, a young woman with dark hair and contrasting blue eyes, whose southern singsong French rang like a happy melody, greeted him. They conferred a minute or two.

"Which one do you think she is?" she asked with an encouraging smile.

PART ONE—EUGÈNE & CARMEN
CHAPTER TWENTY-ONE

Eugène looked around. By this time most of the children were looking at him. He did not wish to disconcert them and was about to seek help from the teacher, when his eyes locked upon a girl who seemed entirely focused on her counting sticks. The teacher nodded happily, "Yes, you're right, that one." She called, "Liliane, come meet your father."

His child came up to the desk slowly. She did not look at him. She was twisting the bottom of her dress into a knot. He felt bad putting her through this—the situation was hard for her.

Someone must have told her something about her father coming to see her soon. But then, the family would have tread as lightly as possible to explain the forthcoming visit. How do you tell a child who loves the family she lives with, that this family is no longer hers?

Liliane reached the teacher's desk and said, "I already got a father, and his name is Papa Dublanc."

She was adorable with her slightly slanted almond eyes, but he saw doubt and a slow kind of fear rising inside them. The teacher appeared to have some sense of this and came to his rescue. "Everything is okay. Show him the way home. I'll see you tomorrow, dear," she told the perplexed child.

Now he was alone with her and did not know what to do or what to say. She let him take her small hand and she led him to *La Capéranie*, her home, protesting all the while that he walked too fast for her short legs. He tried to slow down. He had no idea how to communicate with such a young child. Fortunately, she took the initiative and started talking.

"Stop, stranger, you take giant steps. I am out of breath," she said.

She looked at him for a moment and asked, "Why do you look so sad?"

"I'm not sad," he replied, "it's just that I am so happy to meet you."

She craned her neck and considered him for a second then smiled.

"Did you bring me something?" she asked.

"Oh, yes, some candy and some chewing gum too, for you, and for Fred," he replied, already knowing that, for the rest of their lives, he would have a hard time denying his little girl anything she wanted.

She looked surprised and asked, "Do you know Fred?"

"Yes, I am his father."

"That's funny, I didn't know he had a father. He lives with Madame Duplessy, but I'm sure he'll be happy to meet you."

"You think so?" he asked.

"Of course. And he likes chewing gum too."

He met Monsieur Dublanc in late afternoon. He was a short, ruddy man with a serious but kind face. After inquiring about his health and asking him about his plans, he said with a wink, "Time for us to settle our accounts, Monsieur Grozinger."

They moved into his study. His host went to a desk and pulled a ledger out of it. They sat down. Eugène felt embarrassed—he feared Monsieur Dublanc was about to ask him for money. He had sent small amounts for his children during his captivity whenever he could to supplement the stipend the Association of Prisoners of War gave the host family. At present, he had no money to spare.

"First," Monsieur Dublanc said, "I want you to know that we didn't keep Liliane for money. I was the *maire* of Sabres all through the war. I welcomed our young refugees when they first arrived; my duties included placing them with hosting families."

"Our people work hard. They are cultivators and factory workers. As you can imagine, nobody wanted to take care of a child in

PART ONE—EUGÈNE & CARMEN
CHAPTER TWENTY-ONE

diapers, especially in the summer when planting and harvesting take place. No one wanted to take Liliane. It so happened that my daughters were present."

"'Let us take her home,' they begged. 'We'll take care of her. Look! She is so cute but she looks so sad. See, she's crying. She's just a baby, and she needs a bath. Can't we take her home?'"

Monsieur Dublanc paused for breath and glanced toward the window, his eyes growing distant as he recalled the memory.

"We took her home, and never regretted that decision. She cried a lot; she missed her mother for a long time. One day Paulette found an abandoned kitten and gave it to her. She took care of it, loved it passionately."

"Eventually she accepted us as her family. She has brought much sunshine to our lives. The grandmother spoils her. My wife makes her clothes and sweaters. I make her wooden clogs and wheelbarrows to carry her dolls around."

"She goes to kindergarten and gets good reports. She is friendly and bright and very funny. I assure you we won't mind keeping her as long as you deem necessary. In fact we would be very sad if she left us right away."

Eugène was reassured to hear him say that.

"And when she does return to her family," Monsieur Dublanc continued, "We hope she will come back to visit us whenever she wishes, with your agreement of course."

"Now, as far as money is concerned, I've added the stipends I received from the Association of Prisoners of War to the money you sent me. Here it is. It's all yours."

Eugène was astounded; he didn't know what to say. He searched for words of gratitude, but no sounds came out of his throat.

"That's fine," Monsieur Dublanc said, "You don't need to say anything. We're just repaying part of our debt to you. You fought for France and for us, and we thank you for that. At the same time we grieve for your wife, and hope she is safe and will soon be reunited with her family."

Eugène stayed with the Dublanc family for a few days and basked in their attentions. They fed him their homemade *confit de canard* and omelets filled with fresh chanterelles picked along a stream in the woods. Everything was delicious and graciously offered.

Their care for his family never ceased to overwhelm him. He and his wife had suffered the most inhumane treatment, but here in this neck of the woods lived a family who cared about others. They were the kind of people you are lucky to meet even once in a lifetime. His politics, his religion, or lack of it, didn't interest them. Their backgrounds couldn't have been more different, yet in this time of dire need, the Dublancs had not been afraid to extend shelter and goodwill to this one family who had intersected with theirs. Yet for all this, they were not destined to become great friends. In fact, Eugène never saw them again, though Liliane did each summer, year after year.

During these few days Eugène also attempted to reacquaint himself with his son. He had not expected Fred to forget he had a father. They felt equally awkward with each other.

Eugène thought about Carmen, how if she were in his place, she'd run to embrace her son and cover him with hugs and kisses. He would have to win him back slowly, however difficult that might prove

PART ONE—EUGÈNE & CARMEN
CHAPTER TWENTY-ONE

to be. For now he was taking him back to Paris. Madame Duplessy, his guardian, could no longer keep him. She, too, was returning to the city with her son, Maurice.

"Fred, my little one, don't worry," she told him at supper, "Maurice and I are going back to Paris in a few days. That's where we live, and that's where you will be living too. We'll see each other. Your father has my address. I expect you to come visit me. Will you?"

"Yes, my Aunt. When?"

"Whenever you feel like. Here is my address and my telephone number. I wrote it down for you. You know that I love you very much. Call me whenever you want."

Monsieur Dublanc drove them back to Labouheyre to catch the train for Paris. This time Fred and Eugène carried many packages. His generous hosts had given him a suitcase filled with bed sheets, towels, and washcloths. Madame Dublanc added a large bag with pâtés and preserves. Mamée, the grandmother, also provided candy and chocolates from the stash she kept in a locked armoire.

During the next few months the Dublanc family continued to help them recover. They sent weekly packages. Big or small, they were always welcome. How could Eugène repay the family for the debt he felt he owed them? The only way was to allow Liliane to spend her summer vacations in Sabres. She was always eager to go, though whenever July came around, Eugène tried to entice her to spend her vacation with her Paris family.

"We're going to the Riviera this year. You too, right?" He would ask.

She hated disappointing him, but her answer was always the same: "You know I would, but I have to go to Sabres."

Part Two

LILIANE

Chapter Twenty-Two

When I sat down to write this memoir, I decided I would recount everything I knew and fill in what I didn't. To begin with, I have irremediably effaced most everything that happened to me before age six.

It is as if parts of me fell into a nebula. I can neither see nor retrieve anything from this dark space. Somewhere in its swirling gases resides my early history: my mother's last kiss, her embrace, the arrival by train to a strange place, Fred and I hungry and dirty, the other children equally famished and tired, the transfers by bus, and finally the end of the voyage. Everyone descends willy-nilly from the bus onto Place de la Mairie in Sabres, Landes. Then there is the triage and the separation from Fred. No one among these well-meaning villagers wants a toddler who wears diapers, until Monsieur's daughters, Paulette and Hélène, cry out.

"Look at her, she is so little and so sad. Can't we take her in?"

Maybe that night someone washed and fed me and rocked me until I fell asleep out of sheer exhaustion. The next day I probably awoke still sobbing, calling my mother with the desperation and the stubbornness of a toddler. I wanted her. Where was she?

Among the members of the Dublanc family was an elderly lady with white hair styled in a twist. She said, "*Allons ma petite, ne pleure pas, tu la reverras bientôt ta maman.* [Don't cry, little one. Soon you'll see your momma again]."

This woman became my foster grandmother. She was born in 1871, the year of the Commune uprising (an uprising of workers and intellectuals who rebelled against an autocratic bourgeois government). Her granddaughters called her Mamée, and so soon would I.

I probably adapted to my new family in no time, insouciantly and unconsciously to protect myself. My mother faded, became a shadow, subsided, and finally disappeared. As for my foster father, his name was Papa Dublanc, a ruddy-faced man who always wore his beret until he went to bed. I had never met my biological father, who already was a prisoner of war when I was born.

Taken in by another family, Fred tried to see me. He made several attempts but got lost, or lost his nerve. Then one day he skipped school and walked all the way to *La Capéranie*, the house where the Dublanc family lived. He hid behind the bushes waiting for an opportunity to see me. Papa Dublanc and his daughter Paulette caught him and asked what he wanted. Why hadn't he come to the door for whatever business he may have to transact? He began crying.

"I only wanted to see my little sister," he said miserably.

Papa and Paulette looked at one another. Then Papa Dublanc put a reassuring hand on his shoulder.

"Son," he said, "you're welcome here. Come whenever, but don't cut school. Your teacher won't like that. Who are you staying with?"

"Madame Duplessy," Fred replied.

"Ah, yes, of course, she is a good friend of ours. We'll talk to her. You must come see your sister often. Liliane needs her big brother."

PART TWO—LILIANE
CHAPTER TWENTY-TWO

I was never unhappy in Sabres during the war, or whenever I came there afterwards. On the contrary, and as I grew older and understood what had happened to my family during the war, I felt guilty at my good luck, having had a perfect childhood in a big warm house, with surrounding wheat fields and piney woods, and a complete family of adults who loved me.

As I returned there summer after summer, having read about the terrible fates of people selected by the Nazi machine, I attempted asking questions. I had been told that my mother had come to see Fred and I a few months after our arrival in Sabres. Timidly, I questioned Paulette. "Why did my mother not stay in Sabres with us?"

"Because we were occupied by the Germans," she replied brusquely. "She would have been a danger to us all. Once she came back to the house after curfew. That was a careless thing to do, and we told her so."

This answer upset me. I asked Fred, "Why did our mother go to town and risk missing curfew?"

"To sell some thread and needles or a little lace. She began to exercise this small trade in Paris. She needed to earn some money. She always had great dignity and wanted to pay our host families for the extra things they did for us."

No, I never could understand until now, when I have grandchildren that I am lucky to see grow up. Like all youngsters, they are totally attached to their parents, and particularly to their mother. Between two and three years of age this attachment is total. Once I kept my grandson overnight; more than two or three hours after dark, he began to panic. "I just know, she is never coming back." He was three years old. I tried distracting him, offered to play a game, but nothing helped. Finally, I called my daughter and asked her to come fetch him speedily.

This show of absolute love for 'the mother' makes me regress to my own interrupted childhood. This is what I must have felt as a toddler when my mother was stolen from me; the pain and the abandonment were unbearable, the trauma deep. Something snapped in my young brain, and I lost the memory of the first six years of my life forever.

Chapter Twenty-Three

"Your turn," said Carmen, addressing Berta as if she were present, dusting her photograph in the picture frame. Inside is the portrait of a stern, unsmiling, elderly woman, wearing square dark glasses.

I listened distractedly. Many years later, how I wished I had encouraged her to open up, to give me more details about her life and her experiences. But the girl I was then didn't feel at ease listening to her newly recovered mother's confidences.

"You see," said my mother, speaking to me, "I dust them every day, my mamma's first, even though she was mean to me, then my pappa's. Him, I loved with all my heart. He bought me dresses and hats and chocolates, told me where he had been and what he had seen, took me to see a play or a movie when he returned from business trips. But my mother, that's a different story. She made me her maid, pulled me out of my last year of high school to have me clean house and take care of my sister while she traveled."

"My mother," she continued, "they called her the Belle of Nuremberg. She was a pretty woman, but a haughty, selfish one. She wore enormous hats. They don't make them that big anymore, not even for the queen of England. She wore long silk dresses with black stripes that made her look like a queen bee. My father was also an elegant gentleman."

"They traveled together for business. That's why I had to take full care of my six-year-old spoiled little sister. Sonia made life difficult for me. I didn't much like her; she was a real brat intent on making me miserable. She told lies about me. She said that I brought boyfriends home and that I left her to go out at night. My mother believed her, and I was punished."

"I bided my time—I was only fifteen! I hated both of them and wanted to run away from home."

"Was the brat my Aunt Sonia?" I asked dispassionately.

"Yes. Fortunately, I also had an older brother. His name was Maurice. We loved each other. He looked so much like your brother Fred. He often helped me with the many tasks my mother gave me. That left me free to go sit in the library and return home with books I read late into the night."

"Maurice came to visit us in Paris before you were born, but he died on the train going back to Strasbourg where he lived. Some guys jumped him. Who knows for what reason? He was so young. This was only the beginning of the tragedy to follow."

I listened but did not understand everything my mother was telling me. She spoke to me as if I was an adult, but I was still a child. What was this nebulous tragedy?

I didn't dare ask her to give me examples, though once in a while they popped out of her mouth randomly.

Our apartment didn't have a bathroom. We washed out of the sink during the week and went to the public baths on Saturdays. I remember well the first time my mother took me there. We walked hand-in-hand through the busy streets that led to the establishment.

PART TWO—LILIANE
CHAPTER TWENTY-THREE

My mother paid the cashier. We found the designated bath and took our clothes off. What a shock! My foster family had been very private, and I had never seen a naked human being before.

Mother filled the tub and helped me in; she soaped my back. The water was nice and warm; I relaxed and was having a good time. Yet what I remember most about this day was a feeling of guilt and shame.

We were about to leave when, quite innocently, I asked, "Are we forgetting anything?"

"Only the dirt in the tub," Carmen replied, with a faraway look on her face. Where she went during such moments, I could not follow. I had been happy in the steamy white room, but now I suddenly felt awkward. Had I done something wrong? Was I a dirty child? Was it I who had sent my mother away to those bad places she rarely talked about?

I never knew what to expect from this new, strange mother who often seemed so sad. I coped as best I could, without knowing if I was responsible for her suffering. Guilt hovered over my childhood and my adolescence. I would have to grow up to gain understanding.

But don't imagine for a moment that we children weren't happy in our parents' home. The four of us were born at six-year intervals. The interaction between my brothers and I was positive and nurturing. When Fred practiced his guitar, playing a rondeau or a popular melody, I sat at his feet and listened to him for hours. He was a talent. Sometimes I sang along, mostly some Brassens, Brel, and Aznavour lyrics. They spoke about love, about fleeting youth, about unjustice. Brassens was my idol. He was irreverent, both a poet and a critic. His songs were against the establishment, against war. He sang that no war was worth dying for. All three helped me grow up.

Chapter Twenty-Four

Carmen was wearing her best clothes that day. She looked elegant and exotic with her curly blonde hair and dark green eyes. I had no doubt she was the most beautiful mother in the world. She knocked on the door and, without waiting for a response, entered the classroom. She introduced herself and politely stated the reason for her visit. I was stunned. School and home, like East and West, never met in my mind. Parent-teacher associations did not exist at this time, and the principal, rarely seen, came to a specific classroom only on report card day.

Our teacher was an impatient, unfriendly woman who expected faultless work and prompt answers to her questions. A derelict child who hadn't fulfilled the duties of homework and memorization met her immediate ire.

I had been daydreaming during an oral quiz and did not hear her call my name. "Miss Grozinger, are you asleep? Are you deaf?" she thundered. "Come to my desk, I'll give you a lesson."

I knew the routine and marched to her desk. I braced myself. I would be brave as a Spartan and wouldn't cry in front of her. She bent me over her lap, pulled down my panties and gave me a vigorous spanking.

"There," she said, when she was through disciplining me, "don't let this happen again. Go back to your seat and be alert."

"Class, this is a warning to you all," she added. "Pay attention. Be ready to answer my questions. Indolence is a sign of direspect."

That night was bath time for the Grozinger children. We took turns entering the small tub in which my mother had poured water previously heated on the kitchen stove. I attempted to get in without being noticed, but I couldn't quite hide my enflamed bottom from sight. My mother noticed at once.

"What happened?" she asked.

"I fell at recess," I replied timidly.

"Did someone push you?"

The water was hot and hurt my sore flesh. I wanted to get out and began crying.

"Alright," my mother relented. "Dry yourself. We'll settle this later."

Later was as soon as I got dressed. My mother was waiting; I was forced to confess what had happened in school. And when she appeared there without warning the next day, I panicked. Had she come to give support to the teacher? Would I suffer further punishment? I looked away, trying to make myself smaller than I was. The other children began whispering.

"Quiet," warned the teacher. "Madame," she addressed my mother, "you are disturbing my class. Do you have an emergency?"

"Yes, I do," my mother replied firmly. "You see, I am Liliane's mother, and I'd like you to understand once and for all that I won't have you, or anyone else, strike or hit my child on any part of her body. If it happens again, I will go straight to the principal's office. Physical suffering teaches nothing except fear of other human beings. I'm sure it has no place in any civilized educational institution. This is what I came to say. Good day, Madame, good day, children."

PART TWO—LILIANE
CHAPTER TWENTY-FOUR

My mother left as suddenly as she came. There was a profound silence in the class. After a few moments, the teacher regained her composure and gave us silent reading time for the rest of the afternoon. She must have been shaken; from then on she never again called any child to her desk. She remained icy toward me, but I didn't care. My family would soon be moving to a bigger apartment in another part of Paris, where my brothers and I would attend our respective neighborhood schools.

At home, Carmen said nothing regarding her confrontation with the teacher. What was this physical suffering she'd spoken about? There were so many questions, but I nor my siblings ever dared ask any concerning "the dark years." All my information about the place where her torments had taken place consisted of the cryptic phrases that escaped from her mouth, those lashed out at us in our most unguarded moments. At supper, or lunch, when we left the smallest amount of food on our plates, she'd say without raising her voice, "In Bergen-Belsen, I would have been happy to eat these crumbs off of the lice-covered heads of my fellow inmates."

We didn't like to hear this of course, and took care to consume the littlest crumb with haste. We felt bad and said nothing, though we wanted to know: Why were you sent there? Did you do something bad? What exactly did they do to you? Did you have a bed? Could you brush your teeth? We knew that her world had been a cruel place, and that we were lucky.

On rare occasions, probably after I came back from Sabres, when I was seven or eight years old, I went to sleep in my parents' bed to find refuge, presumably because I was scared. But it didn't help. As soon as I closed my eyes, the mad pursuit began. Some big, faceless thing was chasing an equally faceless, out-of-breath smaller thing. Deep at the center of the turmoil I knew that the little thing was myself, and I awoke feeling not entirely whole, as if some part of myself remained stuck in that nightmare. Could I ever sleep again while the big thing, that monstrous manifestation of evil was trying to catch me?

As I grew older, still rather uninformed about what happened in concentration camps, many were the nights I cried for my mother who had been wronged for no reason. Yet we rarely ever spoke of her war experiences. We were like two land masses separated by a large body of water, bereft of any bridge. Our relationship did not include kissing or hugging; our closest intimacy occurred when she asked me to scratch her back. What emotion I felt when she added, "Look inside the back of my blouse. I feel itchy, some hair must have fallen there." I obliged and felt temporarily redeemed to have lightened the load she carried.

But no, I didn't get it. I understood nothing. She had visited us in Sabres at great peril to herself. She had an intuition, wanted to see us one more time. I didn't remember that visit. Neither did I recall that the Dublancs' opened their house to her when she came back from deportation, so depleted and frail.

I had rapidly repressed all these events as so many fading ghosts in my memory. I even failed to realize that after one, two, three years and more, this stranger I was reunited with had just come back from hell. We children expected her to act normally, as if nothing had happened to her.

She had made all the right decisions concerning her children, even sending them away on faith that strangers could offer them a haven. We lived because of her sacrifice. After that, when she returned from Drancy and Bergen-Belsen (and from Trobitz, as I will relate), there was no one, to my disappointment, in the whole world that could understand or love her enough to remove her pain.

Chapter Twenty-Five

Michel, this round, happy, chubby baby, with no opportunity to endure painful separations, joined a wounded family whom he delighted with his happy personality. By the time Michel was born, Fred was a secretive fifteen-year-old whose religion was soccer and assorted sports. He also practiced classical guitar for relaxation. He finished high school with an honorable mention. Yet because his family was still struggling to make ends meet, Fred's only option was to work and earn a meager salary rather than pursue a college education.

By that time I was nine, and now cannot remember how I felt about the drastic changes that had occurred in my life. I did not remember when we were reunited with my mother, did not remember when my father came for me in Sabres.

I thought my Maman Carmen was too skinny and too preoccupied; besides, she was busy with Michel, the new baby suggested by her physician, who had counseled a rapid pregnancy to rev up his patient's depleted body.

The apartment rue des Tournelles was barely big enough for two people. Suddenly the family expanded; eventually we would be four children and two adults navigating in a small place: Fred and I born before the war then Michel and Patrick born after the war.

Thanks to Elias, my uncle, Eugène and Carmen were alerted about a vacancy in the Marais district. This apartment was only slightly larger than our current one. However, it had more rooms and afforded a modicum of privacy for everyone.

The rooms in the apartment rue des Tournelles were now fully my father's atelier, yet Place des Vosges remained very close distance-wise. Our Francs-Bourgeois apartment also placed us near the rue des Rosiers, the picturesque Jewish neighborhood where tourists and residents now mingle.

The best thing about our new building was the diversity of its quirky inhabitants. The first floor belonged to Madame Hélène, an ageless, disheveled-looking little woman with a perpetual chignon attached to her head. In spite of her street-person appearance, she owned a small grocery store that carried a variety of canned food. There were also vegetables: spinach, carrots, cabbage, and potatoes, and seasonal fruits.

Madame Hélène's produce was not always the freshest, a fact that did not prevent half of her clientele, the retired and elderly people who came daily, to buy her offerings.

Where else would they have the opportunity to shop, chat and rest awhile in this strategically situated boutique, right in the middle of the longish rue des Francs-Bourgeois.

Carmen sent us to Madame Hélène's to buy milk, canned sardines and other small items. She preferred to shop at the Rambuteau, an outdoor market farther down the street.

In the winter, Madame Hélène's boutique became magical. Inside, the soft light attracted a range of customers coming to the

PART TWO—LILIANE
CHAPTER TWENTY-FIVE

shop for a fast purchase or, more likely, paying a visit to its petite commerçante during those late business hours. She favored those lonely people, the *habitués* whose conversations turned animated whether they talked about politics or personal matters.

When the weather turned still colder, Madame Hélène turned up the heat. The grown-ups who meant to stay a little while removed their hats and coats. They sat on the few tabourets Madame Hélène provided. They mellowed, became vulnerable again as they recalled the good and bad days.

"We were tougher then," said a metallurgist with black fingernails, recalling with evident pleasure the daily beatings administered by his father. Those had toughened him, made him defiant, and prepared him for life, especially for the war that, he insisted with pride, turned him into a man.

Michel and I didn't like being beaten—we didn't believe that bad treatment could ever be turned into good. As for war, I, in particular, believed there would never be another. It was all behind us. I survived and would live forever.

One day I returned from school for lunch break and was overcome with a sudden, overwhelming need to drink milk. Carmen, who was not ordinarily the indulgent kind, pulled me inside Madame Hélène's. In those days milk was bought out of a large aluminum keg, then poured into the recycled bottle one rented for a small fee. I drank nearly a liter of milk without stopping.

"My lord," exclaimed Madame Hélène, "she is going to drown!"

"Don't worry," answered Carmen, "I know that feeling. Her thirst needs to be quenched. Let her have more, she'll know when to stop."

That is also what Carmen told Eugène when he happened upon her in their tiny kitchen where she consumed large glasses of water one after the other.

On the second floor of the Francs-Bourgeois building lived the eccentric Monsieur Soulié, a Belgian citizen whose wife preferred to live in Brussels. When she came by, two or three times a year, Monsieur Soulié opened the door of his apartment with a wide gesture of welcome.

"Ma chère," he'd say, "a pleasure to see you!"

Most often, Monsieur Soulié lived with Africans from the Congo who came to France to attend college. He gave them temporary shelter, though in the end, he also adopted one of them.

Kéléfa and he both lived among masks, lances and brilliantly colored faience. Every available surface in the apartment was stacked with books, newspapers, and magazines.

The four floors of stairs Carmen had to climb, sometime more than once daily, were becoming more and more difficult for her to manage. She had to stop and catch her breath several times before reaching her apartment. That's why one day she stopped on the second floor, rung Monsieur Soulié's bell, and introduced herself.

Francis Soulié knew everything about shortness of breath. He had asthma and took relief from a respirator several times a day. He welcomed Carmen inside his apartment where they talked about this and that for about fifteen minutes, after which Carmen got up and said, "See you tomorrow," though she remained at his door some more minutes, long enough to admonish him to get rid of the unsightly piles of newspapers accumulating on the floor of his living room.

Every time she saw him, time and again, she reiterated her advice,

PART TWO—LILIANE
CHAPTER TWENTY-FIVE

"all that old dust is what causes your asthma," to which he always replied, "Ah, ah, ah," together with uproarious laughter that immediately sent him back inside his apartment, choking and searching for his respirator.

Monsieur Soulié loved to chitchat, and one day in the course of their conversation confided to an astonished Carmen that he bought and resold his beautiful antique furniture periodically. "Sometimes," he admitted, "I get bored looking at it, so I sell it and get some new furniture. Nothing is more thrilling than change."

"Whatever!" said Eugène, when he heard that. "He has no children of his own and doesn't know what to do with his wealth. Furthermore, he's never worked a day in his life. He lives on dividends made on the backbreaking work of exploited Africans!"

"You're wrong," Carmen defended him. "He does work. He's a writer."

There were two apartments on the third floor. Monsieur and Madame Goldhamer owned the larger one. Madame Goldhamer was Elias' sister-in-law. She and her husband hardly spoke to anyone. They had a business and owned patents on several models of aprons for children and teenagers. Sometimes they asked Carmen to bring me to their home to test a new model. I was not eager to comply. They were miserly and never said thank you.

"Do it to be polite," Carmen told me.

Years later I lost my American passport while walking on the street in the Latin Quarter. At that time the phone books listed names of telephone owners by building. As it turned out, Monsieur and Madame Goldhamer were the only people who owned a telephone at fifty rue des Francs-Bourgeois. That same day Madame Goldhamer caught Carmen on her way up to her apartment.

"Someone called with a message. Good thing I was home! Your daughter's passport was found," she told Carmen in her Polish-accented French.

One summer the couple invited their nephew from Poland to come visit them. The gossiping in the building intensified. Someone had heard it said that the young man was a mathematical genius. That made a big impression on Michel and me. What did he look like, we wondered. Vladi turned out to be a friendly adolescent who spoke perfect French and seemed not too different from us.

We were not well acquainted with the other couple and their twenty-year-old son who lived in the smaller apartment. We were all surprised when his parents asked Carmen if I would like to accompany their son to a concert. My parents only listened to popular music so the invitation was a great occasion. Of course I wanted to go. It would be the first time I went to a concert, and my primary introduction into the world of classical music. The concert featured the music of Johann Sebastian Bach. His Brandenburg concertos captured my brain and sent it spinning on a higher sphere.

Unfortunately, the young man, whose name I have forgotten, was entertaining romantic ideas of his own. He had been inching close to me and now was pressing his body against mine. I slapped his hand and told him to stop. I came back home unaccompanied and said nothing to my parents. To my relief he left me alone.

My family lived on the fourth floor in an apartment adjacent to the much larger one inhabited by our neighbors, Louis and Hortense Seller.

PART TWO—LILIANE
CHAPTER TWENTY-FIVE

These two had a story. According to Carmen, Monsieur Louis Seller was twenty years younger than his wife, Hortense, who, moreover, was his first cousin. Louis was orphaned when Hortense took him in. She raised him and then proposed when Louis turned eighteen.

That's why Monsieur Seller wore a long white beard, to look as old as his wife, Michel and I thought. We didn't think they were an odd couple. We knew grown-ups did certain things; couples and families had their own arrangements, and that was that.

The Sellers were self-contained but not unfriendly. When we came home from school, if our mother had not returned from errands, we could count on shelter next door. In fact, our neighbors became the nearest thing we had to grandparents. I called Louis "Pépére."

One day at school when I ran to avoid missing the whistle that announced the end of recess, and then tripped abruptly, I fell and broke my arm. My mother was called to come get me. After failing to find a taxi on a busy afternoon, she raised one hand to stop a driver, hauling me all the while with the other. She begged him to take us to a hospital, which after some hesitation he consented to do. My elbow was shattered—I was in great pain. I endured two surgeries followed by daily shots of penicillin. I became a patient at the *hospital des enfants malades* for the next six months. Pépére came to visit me nearly every afternoon, bringing me sweets, books and any thing he thought would please me. But that wasn't all. After my return home he took it upon himself to administer the recommended daily massages to my elbow.

Pépére was in his early sixties. He took care of the apartment and did all the shopping. Hortense, in her eighties, no longer went out. To us, the beautiful old things, the elegant furniture, fine china, and silver goblets they owned seemed out of our reach. In contrast, our parents made do with only secondhand furniture, and only absolutely necessary accessories.

Every day, at some point in the morning, Pépére opened his door. Soon after Carmen did the same. They had finished cleaning their respective apartments and were ready to begin a conversation. Carmen rested her chin on her broom; Pépére held his arm along his door. They loved each other like a sister loves her brother. Their neighborly relationship lasted several years until Hortense died. Then to everyone's surprise, Pépére remarried. He sold his apartment and moved out to a fancy suburb of Paris with his bride, a nurse fifteen years younger than he. Pépére and my mother remained friends and saw each other regularly until he died. Carmen probably confided in him matters she found impossible to tell anyone else. Now in the twenty-first century, I may be the only person who remembers Louis Seller.

Before she died, my mother gave me his photograph. I have it in a frame. At times, I reach for it. Pépére is a handsome older man with a white beard. I imagine that he greets me with a grin and says, "Bonjour, Sarah Bernhard!" because I always spoke of becoming an actress.

Carmen and Eugène retired in the 1970s. They had survived traumatic setbacks, yet through hard work managed to acquire both the apartment in Paris and a small weekend house in the suburbs. Patrick, my youngest brother, still lives in the rue des Francs-Bourgeois apartment.

Carmen missed her Paris friends; sometimes she felt like a prisoner in her suburban home. She also missed the noise and the passersby on her old street in Paris. On the other hand, she enjoyed growing flowers

PART TWO—LILIANE
CHAPTER TWENTY-FIVE

and feeding the many stray cats against Eugène's wishes.

Her entire body hurt during her last years. Her hearing and her sight were affected, and she eventually endured a devastating stroke, recovered miraculously in the course of six months, and lived another ten years, despite clogged arteries and corresponding ailments.

"*Pauvre maman*," I sigh, thinking about her, growing unbearably sad as the day darkens. But I have learned to fight these feelings about the image of my mother as a woman to be pitied. Surely, Carmen enjoyed sweet moments, and loved and smiled, felt proud and lived intensely through her contact with family and friends.

The best portrait of her is one never taken, never framed, yet still fully developed in my memory. In it Carmen stands on the balcony waving her arms at her school-age children, blowing kisses to them with both hands. Whatever the odds, we were a close family.

Chapter Twenty-Six

How many times do you dream the same dream? The road emerges out of a pine forest, becomes rue du Bourg, and speeds to an abrupt end at the town square. There, city hall, school, pharmacy, and movie theater stand, emblematic as chess pieces on a board, the queen of them all, undoubtedly, the church whose ancient steeple announces Sabres from the westernmost approach to the town, seen miles before one reaches it.

Things change slowly in Sabres, except for the steadily declining numbers of jobs. The factory that refined pinesap into turpentine for forty years closed its doors in 1956. The younger citizens now move to the large cities to find work.

I remained "the Parisienne," the girl who stayed with the Dublancs during the war for a long time. With the lilting Southern accent I unsuccessfully endeavored to acquire, they introduced themselves, "Denise! From the Old Mill, at St Michel," "Jean-Baptiste, from the Ouastou, near Commensacq. Knew you when you were nay higher than that, little bitty and scared, just arrived from Paris, with the then-young Miss Dublanc carrying you home on her bicycle seat."

And I was thrilled and grateful. So long as they existed, no matter what anyone else said, these good people validated my place in the enchanted world of a childhood that shines on in my memories.

Pierrette, Paulette's friend, dry goods store owner, town transmitter and repository of gossip past and future, nose curling on its tip into a prominent ball of cartilage, appeared to the child I was like the good fairy godmother of tales. Her knowledge of village lore guided, informed, and prevented the uninitiated me, a Parisian lacking the innate good sense of Sabres' folk, from making such faux pas as shaking the town drunk's hand.

So it is only natural that now, decades older, while in the course of a dream, I turn to a graying Pierrette to find out if the authoritative and judgmental god of my childhood, that Mademoiselle Paulette Dublanc, from the big house known as *La Capéranie*, she who carried me to and from town on her bicycle, changed my diapers, and stopped a nasty big-city cold dead in its tracks after one day's ministrations of certain homemade remedies, has now confided in said Pierrette and related to her the exact nature of the struggle which pitted us against one another one stifling afternoon during my annual visit a few years previous, almost sundering our long, serious relationship.

"Has Paulette told you what happened?" I ask her, hoping to hear that her friend Paulette has reconsidered, thought about what she said to me after going out of her way to provoke me as she did, scolding and belittling me these past thirty years for reasons I cannot fathom until my patience wore out.

Now I rush to tell Pierrette, "Paulette didn't take my rebuke well. You know how she is, proud as a peacock and in her own mind always right. I wouldn't be surprised to hear she's concocted some story to prove to you that after so many years of her care and love, I have proved ungrateful."

PART TWO—LILIANE
CHAPTER TWENTY-SIX

Pierrette's blue eyes get rounder. Any minute now I expect her to shake her head sideways like a parrot that ponders whether or not it should attempt some modicum of communication with the human addressing it.

At that precise moment, I wake up, agitated, murmuring, "You cold bitch, you witch, Paulette. Who do you think you are, treating me like that, at my age? Least you can do is apologize, tell me you're sorry, and hope I'll forgive you."

Problem is, trying to eject Paulette from my dreams, or from my life, isn't easy. The shadow she casts above my early learning years, and even my adulthood, looms as high as the Himalayas. I've loved, feared, and revered her for years, as a needy two-year-old separated by war from her biological family, as an adolescent to whom she appeared severe but, without a doubt, a paragon of domestic virtues: sewing, cooking, knitting, and ironing to perfection. She was also the authority in the household, making definitive comments about Sabres's citizens, about the entire world: "Good-for-nothing Jules," who hunted illegally in her family's woods, who deserved to be shot. Furthermore, she was tired of people who told lies, those who said the rich exploited the poor, that there had been so-called "death camps" in Poland and Germany during the war.

This last remark made Paulette's parents shake their heads and move their eyebrows in warning. When she said that, my mother had only just returned from the infamous Bergen-Belsen concentration camp but a few years previous. The kind Dublancs had registered her physical deterioration after her terrible ordeal, and opened their comfortable, well-provisioned home to her for a few months of healing.

Despite her obvious shortcomings, my faith in Paulette was unshaken; she was the most important person in my life, a close second to my recovered beloved father. She could make order out of disorder, especially in the messy world of politics that adults spoke about. I pictured her ordering assorted miscreants to rake leaves, an endless chore assigned to me during summer visits, which I endured unhappily, all the while comparing myself to the unfortunate Sisyphus repeatedly pushing a jagged boulder uphill.

Paulette's moods made good and bad weather in the big house; she was omnipotent, the guardian of rectitude, the beacon on a dark path, my absolute master who had picked me out from a crowd of children sent out of war-torn Paris to enjoy a few months of calm and fresh air in the countryside. Subsequently, my mother, who was to be arrested a few months later, fearful for my safety, appealed to the Dublancs to keep me with them.

Paulette undertook my upbringing with gusto. She stopped me from biting my fingernails, though in frustration, I surreptitiously began stuffing my finger inside my nose, a much more repulsive habit. Later, when I returned to my parents and Paulette and I corresponded, she sent back my letters after correcting them of the spelling errors and dreadful mistakes in past participle agreements she could never forgive.

But in those days, far from resenting her admonitions or monitoring, I wanted desperately to please her. That was more important than anything else I desired during my passage on earth. Like a vassal, I prayed for the happiness of my lady, hoping she would get married and have children of her own; though I'd certainly be jealous of them.

PART TWO—LILIANE
CHAPTER TWENTY-SIX

My parents parted from me resignedly each summer when I returned to the Dublancs. Two months before vacation, my father spoke about taking his entire family to the seashore. I hated to disappoint him, but I still wanted to go to Sabres. My mother, with her strong sense of obligation, approved with a sigh. "No need torturing the child. She owes them. She must go," she insisted.

The truth is that unconsciously I wanted to be part of the Dublanc family. Paulette and her parents exemplified the kind my own was not: rooted fine old people who lived in the same spot for generations; had scores of relatives spread in numerous villages and counties; did not stick out in a crowd because of attire, manners, or accent; ate the same foods as people around them; whose place of burial was known to them ahead of time; who chose without fear to worship or not; and who lived in a big, comfortable house that, like a person, had a name, an attic filled with the past, and a cellar where fine wine awaited future celebrations.

Chapter Twenty-Seven

I was about to turn eighteeen. My parents were saving money to buy me a round-trip ticket to the United States. It meant I would not spend the next summer with my foster family.

But for the time being, I was on the magic road that connected me to *La Capéranie*, the big house I loved as much as any one of its inhabitants.

We unloaded my luggage from the automobile. Inside the house Paulette immediately opened my suitcase. "Just as I thought!" she exclaimed upon inspecting its contents.

"Our cousins Brouste invited us to the fair. We'll be going to a ball and a musical. Poor child, you've got nothing dressy enough. I'm not taking you there dressed like a gypsy. I better hurry and make you a dress."

She took my measurements and showed me a pattern. "It'll need some adjustments," she warned. "This was meant for a voluptuous body."

Actually, the dress fit perfectly, which made me feel guilty, as if I had willfully wished to contradict my benefactress. Fair day came. I wore the peppermint-striped dress in its crisp glory, aware that Paulette was pleased about her work and her part in rearing me. Whatever maternal feeling she had must be spent on me. She needed me as much as I needed her.

And then I crossed the ocean in the direction Maman Dublanc had once pointed out from the shore of the southwest coast of France, where her family owned a summer home.

"Beyond the water," she said, "is where your grandparents live. Someday you'll surely visit them."

"No, Maman," I replied, "I want to come back here, forever and as long as I live."

"One day you'll marry. You and your family will want to visit other places."

"My own silly girl," she repeated, hugging me. For the first time, noticing her white hair, I was frightened by intimations of my own mortality. "Come whenever you want," she reassured me, "this is your home."

And so it was, even after I moved, married, and settled in the United States. Every time I came to France, I visited the Dublancs. I felt the continuity of their love, how strong mine for them remained despite the forbidding distance between us. And yet something had changed. Everyone was growing older, starting with Grandmother, a wisp of a woman with thinning hair twisted into a small chignon pinned to the back of her head, already old when I first arrived at *La Capéranie*. She had broken her hip and, at one hundred and three years old, was now bedridden, totally dependent on her daughter and granddaughter. The latter, with her usual efficiency, took charge of the old lady. She did her task well but coldly. Grandmother and Paulette had never gotten along. They rarely addressed one another, a situation which had always saddened me, for I loved Grandmother, who never chastised or uttered a harsh word.

PART TWO—LILIANE
CHAPTER TWENTY-SEVEN

She was wildly romantic and read to me from her favorite books by Alexandre Dumas filled with stories of gallant musketeers, priceless jewels, evil bishops and wily queens. She taught me prayers, counted with me from one to ten before turning out lights. We weren't supposed to talk after that. Fortunately, she didn't hold us to the bargain, and told me yet another story.

"Of course she's nice to you, but she's always hated me," Paulette told me when, emboldened one day, I remonstrated with her about her curtness with Grandmother, who in private called Paulette "Sergeant."

And I had changed as well. I had a fifteen-month-old daughter who developed an ear infection on the second day of my visit to *La Capéranie*. The doctor was summoned and prescribed medicine every three hours for the next five days. And that night, Paulette accusatorily pointed her finger at me in front of the whole family. She'd keep the alarm clock by her bedside, she said sternly, "Because, knowing you, you won't wake up to give that poor child her medicine."

"How did I manage without you these past fifteen months?" I heard myself questioning in a firm voice.

This was the first time I had ever stood up to Paulette; she was stunned for a moment, then recovered and practically threw the clock in my face. "From now on, don't expect any help from me," she snapped.

I felt so uncomfortable in her presence I arranged to fly back to my family in Paris the very next day.

Still, during subsequent summers, I came back, now with two children in tow, to say goodbye, first to Grandmother who died peacefully at one hundred and three, then to Papa Dublanc, robbed in his last years of that serenity and contentment he had displayed in his most routine gestures; lastly, goodbye to Maman Dublanc, who underwent the most disturbing psychological transformation of all, from a tower of strength and gentility into a whiny old girl clamoring for Paulette's services, complaining about food—too salty or too tasteless—about the temperature, the roughness of her sheets, and the noise, or lack of it.

Paulette now lived alone in the big house. Her letters, though scarce, were lively and informative. She announced the marriages, births, and deaths of people I knew, recounted her travels abroad, first in the company of a female friend, then when the latter married, with the Sabres Senior Club. I was elated to hear that the *Ecomusée de la Grande Lande* asked her help to classify its archives. That meant she'd have contact with people and something to occupy her during the long winters.

I still returned to visit her, though not without apprehension. No matter that I had reached middle age, that my children were grown, that I had met some of my goals with success, she had a knack for making me feel as worthless as Kafka's Joseph K. awaiting the guilty verdict about to swoop down upon his head.

"Now I have my own car," I told her.

"I wouldn't risk a trip with you," she replied.

Two days later she drove us into a ditch. I didn't press my advantage. She uttered not a single word of apology. But there were also rewarding moments, those I chose to dwell upon, when we shared common remembrances and walked through the pine forest to take a look at her grandfather's old house. We recalled the taste of his lumpy applesauce, repeated to each other the story he loved to recount when he was in the Merchant Marine during World War I and went

PART TWO–LILIANE
CHAPTER TWENTY-SEVEN

around the world, stopping once in a place called Noumea, returning at long last, Ulysses in his creased beret, wanderlust satisfied, never to leave his hamlet again.

I was lulled and lightheaded at those moments, my guard and self-control down. Paulette mentioned her nephew had passed his pharmacy exam. I congratulated her, reciprocating with good news of my own.

"I've finally completed my doctoral dissertation and received my Ph.D. It's the highest academic achievement in the U.S."

"In this country," she replied, "you have to pass the 'Aggregation,' a very difficult exam. Definitely out of your reach."

"Why do you say that?"

"Because you were always a mediocre student. I had to teach you . . . ," she shrugged.

"I know, past participle agreement. For God's sake, I was only twelve. I've learned quite a bit since."

"Be that as it may, only one percent of all students pass the Aggregation. Don't think you're quite in that league."

The exchange left me bewildered. I felt uncertain, humiliated, and indignant.

Back in the U.S., I mulled over the letter I thought I might send her. I composed dozens in my head, stating my disappointment, the chagrin her undue criticism caused me. I thought about mailing her my grades and dissertation, showing her what a fine piece of work my intellect and insights had wrought. But, in the end, I decided to drop the matter. It would have been a waste of time. To begin with, Paulette didn't understand English, and even if she had, she was stubborn and set in her ways. Neither remonstrations nor proofs were likely to change her mind. Despite all, I still loved her because of what she and her family had done for me. I wouldn't allow my anger to tarnish these memories.

A couple of years elapsed before I returned to Sabres. My heart was filled with trepidation as the train brought me closer to my destination. Paulette stood on the platform waving to me, her neck bent by arthritis at an uncomfortable angle.

"Here you are," she said.

We kissed on both cheeks and chatted amiably.

"Must be hard for you to drive with your neck like that," I ventured.

"Takes longer changing lanes, but I'm used to it. There are worse handicaps."

"And how is Hélène?" I asked. Her sister had sent me an announcement, "A grandmother twice!"

"The older child, Jacques, is terribly spoiled. And you'd best not say anything in front of the parents. Last time they were here, he broke one of my good Limoges plates."

"Really, what did you do?" I asked with interest.

"Nothing. Jean-Paul told him to be more careful."

I thought Paulette's nephew, Jean-Paul, must have been the first person ever to put fear in her heart.

The next day went well. We took our walk through the forest, paid our respects to Grandfather's house. In the evening we watched Paulette's favorite game shows, French versions of "Wheel Of Fortune" and "The Dating Game." We played a little Scrabble, drank warm milk, and retired to bed.

PART TWO—LILIANE
CHAPTER TWENTY-SEVEN

On day two, I made my pilgrimage through town. The beautiful church with its wafer-thin steeple had been restored. Inside the air was redolent of the acrid smell of incense. I sat at a pew, recollecting indelible scenes from my childhood: Papa Dublanc with his unbelieving friends awaiting a funeral procession from his post at the café across the church, raising his glass of wine to the deceased's memory; myself not of the faith, happy to go in for the "Great Mass" when the choir sang Gregorian chants.

I walked to the cemetery and found the Dublancs' mausoleum. "See," I told Papa and Maman—Papé and Mamée—recalling each in turn as if they still lived, "I will always come back."

"You didn't go to Pierrette's?" said Paulette when I told her what I had done in town. "You passed by her shop without going in to say hello?"

"She was busy with customers. You said we were going to visit her this afternoon."

Here were the first clouds. We ate lunch in silence. Fortunately, the afternoon at Pierrette's went well. As usual she peppered me with questions without giving me anytime to answer.

"Look at you! Haven't changed a bit; not even a white hair! And you still live that far, all the way in the United States? Tell me have you seen J.R.? How many horses has he got? They have guns and big hats in Texas, don't they? Bang, bang! And your children? Probably pretty big by now? Sit down, you're in no hurry. Let's talk, I'll make us some tea."

Day three: Paulette wanted to go to Mont-de-Marsan, a relatively big town, to buy herself a white blazer. We got into the car steaming under the sun. I rolled the window down an inch.

"Close it," said Paulette peremptorily, "you're letting hot air in."

Back at *La Capéranie*, Paulette turned on the TV. I sat seething with repressed anger, silently vilifying her with dozens of choice epithets. It was then that she made some innocuous comment followed by a slight but sarcastic remark, the nearest equivalent of which can be best translated as "still hot under the ears?" No doubt this set me off and ignited the conflagration that would alter our relationship for some time.

"Shut up!" I said, hardly believing I was talking to her like that. "You've been insulting me for years. I've held my tongue until now, but this time you've passed the limit. I'm grown up; I'm forty-five years old. No one speaks to me that way, not even you."

"Oh! Madame is angry with me?"

"You bet I am. I'm not a kid anymore. You can't boss me around. You show neither regard nor respect for my feelings. And don't think I've forgotten what you said to me two years ago when I told you about my degree."

"Yes, I remember clearly. I meant every word I said."

"What you think is one thing, what you say is quite another. I might think any number of things about anyone, including you, but I don't have to tell you. You don't need to go about hurting people, least of all those you're supposed to love."

"So, that's why you've stayed away so long. You didn't have the guts to face me. And while we're being honest, let me tell you, I'm sick of your constant bragging."

"Bragging? Since when is sharing your success with a loved one bragging?"

PART TWO—LILIANE
CHAPTER TWENTY-SEVEN

"Wanting to buy an apartment in Paris! As if you could afford one!"

"And why not? You know nothing about my finances!" I shouted. "It's my dream! If you had one, however improbable it might be, I'd say go for it and good luck to you."

"You never dared to talk to Maman in that tone of voice."

"Leave her out of this. She knew how to love. She wasn't afraid to praise when praised was deserved. But that's not the point. I didn't come to visit you to have a fight. I'll leave tomorrow, and that's not soon enough for me!"

We ate in silence. I helped clear the dishes and retired to Grandmother's old room.

"See," I said addressing her memory, "see what Paulette's done?"

"Sergeant," I laughed, remembering Grandmother's name for Paulette. I clicked my heels and gave a mocking salute. No, I wasn't that upset. In fact, I was in the throes of cathartic glee, feeling light and free, as if I'd finally gotten rid of a bothersome hair shirt. I climbed into Grandmother's bed and turned out the lights.

The clock struck eleven times. Suddenly I was a little girl scared of the dark and of the wind blowing outside. This was such a big, isolated house. I heard Paulette rambling upstairs, listened for a creak of footsteps down the stairs. I tried counting to ten. The futility of that device whipped my fear into frenzy. What if my old god upstairs was plotting revenge? I leapt out of bed to check my door. The lock was stuck; the key refused to turn. I dragged an armchair in front of the door. Should anyone seek entrance during my sleep, the noise would wake me.

"You're insane," I told myself. "She may be cold and cruel, but she isn't going to hurt you."

Reason seldom suffices when the mind panics. In Paris I had bought the small Opinel folding knife my husband asked me to bring back. I pulled it out of my purse, checked the blade, and put it under my pillow. I wouldn't leave this world without a fight, a promise I made to myself when I understood what had happened in the place where the Nazis took my mother.

On the train leading me away from the cherished kingdom of my childhood, I reviewed the events leading to the rupture I'd tried so hard to avoid.

But I wasn't through with Paulette. Eventually, I wrote and mailed her the letter I had composed so often in my mind. I didn't expect her to reply, and she didn't. But if she read it anyway, as I hoped she would, she might have heard, in spite of the harsh truths delivered, "I love you and care about you."

And that is my ongoing revenge. Every three months or so, I write, inquiring about her health, giving her news, saying, "It's me, I exist. No matter what, whether you want it or not, we are connected to each other."

And when the dream returns, I'm transported, bathed in light: road, pines, town square, *La Capéranie*, potted geraniums under the sun. I walk to the front door, stand there until Paulette opens. She looks at me atop her tilted neck. "So, it's you," she says in her impatient voice. "What are you waiting for? Why don't you come in?"

I hesitate, and when I finally make up my mind to cross her threshold, my beating heart awakens me.

Chapter Twenty-Eight

What was it like growing up with Carmen? Nearly hell, if it hadn't been for my father, who adored his only daughter, who took time to talk to her about politics, about the books he read, about the conversations he had with his clients; otherwise I am not sure what the answer to that question might have been.

He was my mentor—I learned so much from him; first to become a good listener and, more importantly, to question and stay on my guard. Sometimes he'd warn, "don't be a dumb woman," and at others, "Watch out, the women in our family turn to fat." These were the dreaded pitfalls I swore to avoid during my lifetime.

There was no school on Thursdays. Every Wednesday evening, Father and I went to the movies, arm in arm, like lovers. After the film ended, we analyzed the plot and the actors' gestures as well as the tone of their voices.

"In the end," Father said, "everything is political. The way the actors dress, how they speak, their accent, what and how they eat, the music that surrounds the action, the colors, etc."

Most of the American movies we viewed were subtitled in French; even so I loved the sounds of English and tried to concentrate on the spoken words while reading their translation in French. I began studying English in high school. Though I had missed the first part of the year because of illness, I caught up fast. By the end of the school year, I was making the best grade in the class.

Many of my schoolmates went to the cafeteria for lunch, but that was not compulsory. There was an hour-and-a-half recess before class resumed. Michel and I ran home together, sometimes to be greeted by the wonderful odor of sauerkraut our mother cooked. Our kitchen window opened onto the staircase. We could hear her singing *Beltz, Mayn Shtetele Beltz* in the tiny kitchen. The sad tune with its melancholy melody sang of elsewhere and stood as an emblem of what it was like living in a village before it became *Judenrein*.

But at other times, especially at the end of the school day, I began to worry and walked up to the sixth floor slowly, wondering if and praying my mother would be in a good mood. Carmen could turn violent at times. Once she chased Fred round and round around the apartment, brandishing a wooden spoon with which she intended to hit him. He ran faster than her. Then she stopped, panting from sheer exhaustion. Fred came toward her and helped her calm down. She had a weak heart. Gently he said, "Go ahead and hit me with that spoon."

Fred turned twenty. He left home and married his girlfriend Jeanette. Six months later he was conscripted into the army. I was now the eldest child at home, always on my guard, trying my best to avoid displeasing my mother

It was my duty to pick up the mail six floors down in Madame Chevalier's tiny ground floor apartment. Madame Chevalier was the concierge and a long-time widow. She and I were friends. I knocked on her door every day. She always opened it with the same mantra,

PART TWO—LILIANE
CHAPTER TWENTY-EIGHT

"Bills for your parents, a letter for Fred; it will have to be forwarded. But nothing for you! Your boyfriend is forgetting you."

"Madame Chevalier, I don't have a boyfriend," I'd reply.

One day she crowed, "Guess what?" She was hiding something behind her back.

I turned red and replied, "Did I get a letter? Well, give it to me, but please don't tell my mother. I met a young man at the Hungarian volleyball club. He asked if he could write me. He is smart, nice, and cute. I said yes."

"Don't worry," she reassured me, "once I was as young as you are, even if it's hard to believe. It's not as if you were plotting a crime."

The tone of the letter was sweet and polite. Jean-Claude and I met in a café; we spoke about our goals, our hopes. We laughed, arranged another date. In the meantime his letter sat in my pocket. I read it over and over again, but I was careless. It fell out of my pocket without my noticing. Carmen found it and read it.

She was infuriated. Going out with a boy without her or my father's knowledge! And though I was nearly eighteen at the time, she beat me with a belt. I was stunned. She was hurting me. I begged her to stop. Michel tried to intervene; she pushed him away. He was twelve and could only scream, "Stop, stop!" She did eventually, and then threatened to tell my father. I should have told her to go ahead and do so. I was sure my father would not condone her behavior.

I don't remember how I lived the next few days in the apartment. I did not like what my mother had done, but I did not hate her. I pitied her and managed to love her for different reasons. Carmen had suffered unfairly and unimaginably, that's why I forgave her. We never talked about that incident again.

The following year my parents sent me to the United States to visit my extended family in America. For the first time in my life I found myself alone on a boat sailing across the ocean in the midst of strangers. The five-day voyage aboard the Queen Mary provided me with absolute freedom and unimagined amenities: a deck on which to observe obsessively both the ocean and the passengers, my own cabin, and a well-stocked library. Add to that splendid meals three times a day. I made the acquaintance of young people my age. On the last day we greeted the imposing Statue of Liberty, and promised to stay in touch with each other. We did for a while, then stopped when life continued to pull us in opposite directions.

    After a brief visit in Connecticut with my aunt Sonia and her family, I flew to Dallas, Texas, adding another new experience to the events of my life. First, there had been the vast ocean with untamed waves, and now pillowy clouds large and small, floating through space by my window like a mirage.

    My uncle Fred Time and his wife, Judith, were waiting for me. They gave me a warm welcome. It was difficult to reciprocate. I felt awkward, unsure of my English.

    They immediately drove me to meet Judith's family. There, I was introduced to a young man named Harvey Richman, who looked like James Dean. I was barely nineteen when we married; he was a year older—I had only known him for a couple months. I was happy and sad at once: how could I leave Paris, my beloved city, for Dallas, Texas, where people hardly ever walked? It seemed there were twice as many cars as people; consequently, there was little public transportation. I did not know how to drive and was often stuck home.

PART TWO—LILIANE
CHAPTER TWENTY-EIGHT

One day I tried to take a walk around my neighborhood and was stopped by a policeman who asked me what I was doing. He looked surprised when I explained that I was just taking a walk. This was Dallas in the late fifties. Why exert yourself when you could drive?

I was homesick, unhappy, lost, and unoccupied. I considered returning to Paris but realized there would be difficulties. In the balance weighed several considerations. Where would I go and what would I do if I returned home? My education consisted of a diploma in accounting, but I had neither previous job experience nor any money to my name. More importantly, I could no longer face living with Carmen.

Today, I am sure I made the right decision though my conscience still aches. The charges I brought against myself stood as abandonment and desertion, leaving my parents, my brothers, my country, Sabres and Paris. All and all, I had lived only eleven years with my parents. Carmen and I would never live and evolve together as adults. Of course I came back to visit, but we never confided anything of much importance to each other. One summer, however, Carmen took me aside. She had something to tell me.

"Let's go visit Fred and Jeanette," she said. "We'll have time to talk on the train, just you and me. Your father always monopolizes the conversation. I can't compete with him. Of course, I know that you'd rather talk with him."

"Don't say that; it's not so," I protested, though she was right. My father was a force of nature as far as conversation was concerned.

"No, it's true," she replied, "but I've made my peace with that."

So we went, but said nothing to each other. Carmen was tentative and could not find the words. She was an ill woman who wore a pacemaker; her body was slowly abandoning her. I did not press her, but I should have. It was my duty as a daughter to know everything, even the unspeakable. I didn't stand up to the task and once more experienced paroxysms of guilt.

Chapter Twenty-Nine

After receiving the second highest score for the *Certificat d'etudes* in the fourth arrondissement of Paris, Fred became a mere laborer in the tailoring trade, assembling as many pairs of sleeves and pants as possible in a work day.

"Entirely my fault," Fred admitted when I questioned him a long time after the fact. "Soccer was the only thing that interested me. I could have played all day long; I forgot everything else. You remember when we went to school at Place des Vosges? I played in the park before and after school, sometimes until dark. My friends looked out for me and warned me, 'Watch out, Fred, your father is coming!'

"When I was fourteen, I vaguely wanted to be a sportswriter, but it was too soon after the war, our parents didn't have the money, and I didn't push them. Father found a tailor to show me how to work the sewing machine. I did piece work for him. It wasn't demanding, but it was boring. I consoled myself by taking evening classes at the Music Conservatory. I played the classical guitar and earned a second place in the annual competition, but I knew I could not become a full-time musician. I had to work until I couldn't stand it anymore." That's when he went to night classes to study management. After that, Fred opened his own atelier and hired six employees. There was plenty of work and increasing profits for the next ten years. Then came the crash of the 1970s, and he went bankrupt. Fred never imagined he would be jobless in his fifties.

Like many others, he applied for a government job when his business failed. It would not be easy. There was a paucity of those.

I remember the day he was supposed to find whether or not he would be the lucky recipient of a government position. He, Jeanette, and I were on vacation in Brittany. We were walking along the sea to a public telephone amidst wild wheat and red poppies. It was Jeanette's idea; she thought the exercise would allay the tension of the moment. Fred, ahead of us, was dialing the phone. We stopped behind him and observed his gestures. He was talking, nodding, and shaking his head up and down. At one point, he seemed to be listening for a long time without replying. We might have been more nervous than he. He finally hung up the phone, and we ran to meet him. Would we hear good or bad news? Was he smiling? It was hard to tell. Then suddenly he exploded in laughter.

Yes, he had gotten the job. We kissed and hugged him and asked many questions.

"What exactly is this job about?" Jeanette and I asked.

"I will be teaching management wherever the government sends me. My first destination is Tunisia," he said. "And Jeanette can travel with me."

At age fifty-five Fred took advantage of a clause in his contract that offered him time to study, free of charge, for an advanced degree in whatever field he desired. It took him three years to do research in psychology, write a thesis, and be awarded a master's degree.

The preface to his master's thesis, entitled *Relationships Between*

PART TWO—LILIANE
CHAPTER TWENTY-NINE

Grown-up Children and Their Aged Parents, relates the struggles of our parents and the peril they encountered in their daily lives during the war years, as well as the toll taken on my mother's health during her incarceration. Fred was definitely Carmen's favorite child. I always thought that he loved her deeply and had a special rapport with her. Yet, in his aforementioned preface Fred indicates that just like me, he shared powerful feelings of guilt caused by his inability to love Carmen as he should have.

He portrays her as a rather simple woman, without education or interests. But Carmen had almost finished high school. She spoke three languages: German, Yiddish, and French; and even learned a little English. She read multiple sections of the newspaper and had opinions. She was not afraid to contradict Eugène, who could be authoritarian and didactic.

The proof of that is engraved in my memory. It occurred the day my father came home from work with a gloomy face. Comrade Stalin had just died. Eugène seemed devastated, in deep mourning for the dictator he'd admired during the war and for some time afterward. It would take him decades to admit that Stalin had inflicted a murderous dictatorship upon the Russian people.

That night, someone at the supper table made some innocuous remark to which my father responded with inappropriate anger. Everyone was shocked by Eugène's rage; a deep silence fell upon the family. It ended when Carmen spoke these words: "Your Stalin was nothing but a criminal on a grand scale. Any leader who finds the need to parade giant portraits of himself ends up crushing his people. I'm glad the bastard is finally gone. We don't need to mourn for him."

Her words struck the table like lightning. All of us children forgot to breathe. We thought our mother had gone too far and would be instantly incinerated in the fallout. Instead, silence continued to weigh the small room down. We ate in a hurry and scampered to bed, not even daring to whisper to one another.

Chapter Thirty

From Fred's preface to his master's thesis:
I was born in Paris to a family originating in Eastern Europe, the eldest of four children who underwent a difficult childhood and adolescence.

Before the war my parents had already faced all the difficulties inherent to their status of immigrants, rendered even more precarious because of their Jewish roots. During the war the denigration and vilification of Jews across Europe increased a hundredfold and, like many other families, my parents became prisoners of their era. Cast away with few alternatives for survival, Jews were forced to leave their native countries. They fled wherever they could to start their lives again, in the Americas, China, or India, wherever a door was open. Others clung to diminishing hopes of peace and remained to face adversity. Many were assassinated in their own country; others fought and perished, suffered, or survived at great cost. My parents' fortunes ebbed within that context.

When I was six years old, World War II began. My father enlisted in the French army. My mother, whose family had immigrated to the United States in 1938, found herself alone and pregnant. She gave birth to my little sister in the middle of this chaos.

I remember walking with her to the hospital on a dark and cold day accompanied by rain and distant sounds of bombs. Because I was a child, I was denied entrance to the hospital and returned to rue des Tournelles alone. Our neighbors, Monsieur and Madame Raby, who were childless, did their best to help me. They fed and lodged me, but could not prevent my escaping to the hospital whenever I felt like. It was too difficult to argue with the hospital personnel and persuade them to let me in to see my mother and the new baby. Most times, I entered the back of the building or stood on a slippery pile of coal outside my mother's window. We threw each other kisses, and my mother signaled with her fingers the number of days left until she'd return to our apartment.

In 1942 I was eight-and-a-half years old. My two-year-old sister and I left Paris to seek refuge in Les Landes, a region situated in the southwest of France. We stayed there in separate homes until the end of the war, surrounded by the care and affection of our adoptive families.

My mother remained in Paris and was soon arrested and deported to the Bergen-Belsen concentration camp in Germany. My father was now a prisoner of war, also in Germany. For the child I was then, the breakup of our family and its unacceptable reasons tore me apart. The memory of that period remains forever engraved in my heart. I still feel the unbearable suffering that assailed me, and the shame mixed with rebelliousness that controlled most of my actions. Today still, the remembrance of these dark years weighs on me, occasioning in me the strange pride of those who have walked through fire and survive to tell about it. I remained angry into adolescence because history had roughly shaped my destiny. Later, I made up my mind I would be the one who shaped and controlled the rest of my life.

PART TWO—LILIANE
CHAPTER THIRTY

I grew up hidden until 1945. My father returned from captivity and came back to retrieve us from the homes of the good people who had saved us from peril. By then I was eleven. I recall our fumbling, feverish reunion, the occurrence of which I did not comprehend. My father and I went to find my little sister, who was in kindergarten. This would be the first time he ever saw her. She ran toward me and kissed me, ignoring my father, a stranger, until forced to acknowledge him. I will never forget this scene: the tears, my father's happiness, my sister's total incomprehension and her visible fear. Who was this stranger marked by hardship and who insisted he was her father?

Then my mother came back. I cannot describe her mental and physical state. How was it possible for a child to understand the distress and the humiliation in her eyes, the deterioration of her body and of her face that no longer appeared entirely human?

She still keeps the stigma of her sojourn in hell. Her heart cannot beat without the help of a pacemaker. She is haunted day and night by the unspeakable. Her mind cannot erase the intolerable memories that continue to mar her life. However life goes on; my two brothers were born after the war.

My father worked from 7 a.m. to 7 p.m. In the evening he talked animatedly and told many stories. I marveled at his tales, his unleashed imagination weaving together the traditions of his native home life in the village of Tyukod, Hungary. He described his hopes and desires, recounted his disappointments, passions, and regrets, and evoked childhood remembrances. He recalled his home life and the Jewish celebrations during holidays. At times, he reported the horrendous events he witnessed during war and captivity, imbuing them both with a dose of humor and self-deprecation. One day, he said, he was famished, and by luck found several bars of chocolate. He gulped them up, one after another, only to experience a horrible bout of constipation lasting for several days. And lo and behold, when he finally excreted the matter, it had the appearance of the original chocolate. We laughed and laughed about that. It became my favorite story, as magic and awesome as any Grimm's fairy tale.

Even with the lack of any lengthy school education my father had vast knowledge and an intellectual demeanor. He read incessantly and discussed politics with his friends and clients in a lively manner. It is to him I owe my knowledge of what is important in life. Also from him was born my thirst for knowledge and discovery. My father, now in his seventies, preserves a youthful searching, an unending curiosity and a concern for contemporary events.

My mother, on the other hand, never seemed to recover her prewar *joie de vivre*. Like my father, she had little formal education. She was a woman living in an era when most females were relegated to their homes. She shopped and cooked three meals a day and liked to stay home in the evenings. She never read anything beyond the newspaper my father brought home. The horrors of war had stultified her mind and her heart, hardened and isolated her. She was unable to dispense warmth and love, and her children could not begin to understand her. I felt ill at ease facing her; also guilty, as if somehow I was responsible for her suffering. I still blame myself for not supporting her, not showing her enough love and affection.

Now I have my own family and two grown children. My wife and I have tried to raise them in a free atmosphere with a few solid principles,

PART TWO—LILIANE
CHAPTER THIRTY

among them the support of justice for all and against segregation of any people, anywhere. We have given our son and daughter all the love we are capable of, the love that was lacking during our stolen childhood. We both know loss, my wife having been robbed of her father, who was beaten in her presence during the last days of the war, then arrested, deported, and shot in Silesia, his final destination. During his deportation, he wrote a letter to his family that he handed to a railway employee, who cared enough to deliver it. Jeanette possesses it to this day. We teach our children to understand "the other." We hope they will be thirsty to learn, to discover, to celebrate life.

Chapter Thirty-One

The neighborhood kids of hardworking parents from the lower classes living in the Marais, an area that was not yet the chic quarter it has become, were sent to elementary schools from which we graduated at age fourteen with or without the *Certificat d'études*. This diploma signaled the end of our primary education and our entry as workers or apprentices into the marketplace of the postwar years. My brothers one after another would follow this track.

I had a good voice, wanted to be a stage actress, a singer, or perhaps a writer. Michel read my diary and wanted me to write something about him. He saved his money to offer me a Waterman fountain pen for my birthday. I thought it was a present meant for a queen. When I much later began doing some office work for one of my father's friends, I reciprocated and bought presents, chocolate and pastries for Michel, flowers for my mother.

What to do with me, then, at age fourteen? This matter and its resolution came to a head at the end of 1954 on the day Carmen and Eugène walked to my school for their teacher-parent conference. Their ambitions for their children were limited. They expected their offspring to learn a trade and make a living as soon as possible, as Fred had done by taking a menial job. Fresh out of elementary school, he remitted a portion of his earnings to my parents for room and board. Life was difficult for a family of six with a sole wage earner.

What kind of job could I obtain at my age anyway? I had no desire to learn a trade or to become apprenticed like Fred. I hated anything having to do with sewing, and I already considered myself an intellectual, though I didn't exactly understand how to become one. I knew I wrote the best papers in the class. I also excelled in spelling, geography, and history. Literature was my passion, and theater my chosen vocation, my declared goal.

My teacher, Mademoiselle Deschamps, always encouraged me; she insisted that I should pursue secondary education. She said that I had good grades, was gifted, and deserved to go on to high school. High school began at age twelve, and I was past thirteen. I had missed a year and would have to catch up on my own to stay with my age group. I was eager to follow my teacher's advice, but first my parents must agree to let me pursue my education.

My parents and I met with Mademoiselle Deschamps one afternoon after school to discuss the situation. The adults began talking about me while I sat tense and remote. There was a buzzing in my ears; I could not concentrate. Then, as if some magic button had been pressed, I was pulled out of darkness like a baby experiencing birth—stuck somewhere between the reality and unreality of it all—sensing my entire future was at stake.

My parents were still debating my fate, when eventually my father looked at me, his only daughter; he was suddenly inspired. "Look at her hands!" he told my mother. "They're too small to do manual labor. She can't even turn the key in the lock of our door. Sewing is

PART TWO–LILIANE
CHAPTER THIRTY-ONE

not for her. I believe we must send her to high school."

I was ecstatically happy when I heard this verdict. I thanked my parents profusely and did more than my share of chores in our home to show my appreciation.

I remember my pounding heart on the first day as I pushed open the imposing door of Geoffroy l'Asnier High School. How would I fit in with my new classmates? They had already completed a year of English. Fortunately, the teacher began reviewing most of what had been taught during the preceding year. I listened attentively, repeated what I heard. It was like a game; I caught up fast. Each time I spoke English, I imagined myself an actress learning to view life through the window of this foreign language. I was determined to succeed and did in most subjects, except in math.

Madame Caillat, our sadistic math teacher, walked into the classroom every other day, looked at us for an instant, then greeted us with a lugubrious voice: "Close the door! Open the window! Take out a piece of paper!" she said all at once. The majority of us, except for the few nerds who loved and excelled in math, were resigned—we would fail most of her tests.

She insisted that I understood geometry but did not apply myself. Yes, I told her, I could write down the hypothesis, but the process that led to the proof eluded me.

She could have tried to explain, but that was not her method. "I know you can do it," she repeated, "try harder." Unfortunately, Madame Caillat also taught algebra. She enjoyed giving us short oral tests without any prior warning. They were as lethal as tornadoes and sucked the air out of our throats. She expected immediate answers to her rapid-fire questions and gave us zeroes, minus ten, minus twenty.

She called my name; I half opened my mouth. Madame Caillat shut it down before I could utter a sound with a resounding, "Zero!" I was frozen out of math. I was pleasantly surprised years later to discover that algebra wasn't really that difficult.

In the inner courtyard, at recess, morning and afternoon, friendships were cemented and rivalries dissolved. Jeanette Avergon was my friend. I studied with her after school in her family's apartment. They had a TV! Jeanette was an only child who received significant pocket money. She was one of the wealthier kids in our all-girl class. Unlike me, she had been admitted to high school at the proper age.

My rival was Monique Zanditenas—another privileged girl, who I imagined was never sent to the cellar to bring back a bucket of coal to warm up her family apartment at night, as Michel and I did. Monique Z. and I were competitors, striving to win the best part for the play to be performed at the end of the year. I, in my immodest way, knew I was by far the better actress. Indeed, I always got the best part.

One year I played the miser in Molière's eponymous play and received the acclaim of a spirited public of parents and friends. In their applause, I heard future success and the promise of a career.

Chapter Thirty-Two

Most every one in my high school harbored dreams, as had previous generations, including those students who had been between fifteen and eighteen years old in 1940. Those Geoffroy l'Asnier students, however, had the misfortune to grow up in the wartime years. Many were daughters of immigrants fleeing to escape poverty and discrimination. Most came from Eastern Europe and settled in the Marais, an area already heavily populated by Jewish families.

This school felt like a nurturing home, one I loved passionately because of the education I felt so privileged to receive. It was here at this school, however, that the police came to arrest Jewish children during the war. All perished far away from their homes and were seemingly forgotten and unaccounted for—their deaths never recorded in our history books. Nor was any plaque engraved with their names to remind the passersby of the terrible fates they met. It was as if the recent past was obliterated. There was no time for it, even for those, like my parents, who had survived. Instead, everything echoed to the tunes of recovery, normalcy, and good times, as suggested by the song our music teacher taught us: "Oh we are so lucky to be boys and girls in a country where everything begins and ends with a song."

Five decades later, acts and facts finally began to be acknowledged under the tenure of President Jacques Chirac. His speech about the Vichy government shocked those of us who had constantly heard their politicians affirm that the collaboration with the German occupiers was an aberration.

"No," protested Chirac, "Vichy was France. The president of our republic at the time, Maréchal Pétain, was French. French government employees staffed his administration from top to bottom. Their political choices, and their crimes are part of our history. They shame us and we must atone."

Finally after Chirac's declaration, the city affixed a heart-rending plaque to the wall of a kindergarten in the rue de Rosiers to commemorate the arrest and deportation of Jewish children and their teachers.

In 2003 I went to an exhibit organized by L'Hôtel de Ville, the main city hall of Paris. It showed many documents attesting to the organized terror that took place against the Jews living in the Marais. Many of the deported girls bore my first name—Liliane being a popular name at the time. Had I been older, I could have been any one of them, tossed aside in the maelstrom of the times.

Much of the information displayed in the exhibit had already been made available to the public through the indefatigable work of individuals, such as the lawyer Serge Klarsfeld, who compiled lists of the names of deportees, the dates of their arrest, and the numbers assigned to their convoys out of France on the way to death camps. My brother Fred purchased that thick book. It was filled with names both foreign and French. Visiting Paris in 2006, I viewed them on the Shoah Memorial, a monolithic monument of tall black granite slabs, truly a national memorial.

During that same visit, my uncle Fred Time, Carmen's much

PART TWO—LILIANE
CHAPTER THIRTY-TWO

younger brother, accompanied me to the Shoah Memorial and the Center for Contemporary Jewish Documentation, located at rue Geoffroy l'Asnier, right across from my old high school.

We were looking for Carmen's name, one among the approximately sixty-eight thousand persons deported from France, some who came back and many who did not.

The day was humid and treacherously warm. We craned our necks trying to locate one name among so many and were soon discouraged. The walls stretched into rows, and in order of year of deportation; but I had forgotten the exact year Carmen's transport left Drancy for Bergen-Belsen. The sun was slaying us between the eyes. The names of the deportees, etched so close to one another, clamored for our attention. Ill at ease and increasingly vulnerable, I felt trapped in their numbers, squeezed, pushed, and crushed by this crowd of unfortunates. It was stifling. I nearly fainted and had to sit down. My uncle Fred took me to a bench in the shade and gave me some water.

"She is not here," I told him, feeling miserable. "They've forgotten her."

"Let's go inside the information center. They'll tell us where she is," he suggested.

The employee in service pulled out a slim folder and gave us copies of the document inside. The name of the city mentioned where Carmen's liberation took place popped up—a sudden slap on my face. "Trobitz, or Urobitz?" I cried out. "Which is it? What is it? Where is it? My mother never said anything about such a place. She only spoke about Drancy and Bergen-Belsen."

The employee shook his head. "I don't know," he said. "I've

never heard that place being mentioned before."

Trobitz bore into me and remained an enigma for several months. It was difficult to decide whether the first letter of this unknown place started with a "U" or with a "T." Finally a German speaker confirmed the "T."

Still, Carmen had always insisted that the Russians had liberated her at Bergen-Belsen. She recalled being afraid of them. Some of the soldiers, men with slanted dark eyes wearing furs, were said to rape women.

It is widely known that the British liberated Bergen-Belsen. The stories about Russians raping the sick and broken women they just liberated from the Germans made no sense. Everyone in my family thought that Carmen was mistaken about these facts, that at the time of her liberation she was already so stricken with typhus and dysentery, she was not really aware of what was going on around her.

But indeed, the recently published memoirs I was reading mentioned incidents connected to the arrival of the Cossacks in Trobitz. They describe their appearance and their furry hats, and how the Russian commanders who accompanied them disciplined the culprits for the improper acts they committed.

What and where was Trobitz? I turned to my friend Jacques Waisemberg, himself a hidden child who knew Fred in Sabres, to do some research for me. He provided an article that contained a text written in German that seemed to describe some plan for the building of a commemorative monument. I was puzzled and still felt the ruminations of an unsatisfied hunger to know exactly what had happened during this last chapter of my mother's torments. Without further elucidation, I

PART TWO—LILIANE
CHAPTER THIRTY-TWO

felt I would lose her forever, even though she was no longer alive.

My daughter began searching the Internet and found material of interest. I was shocked by its content, but also strangely satisfied to discover what had been my mother's fate in these last critical days of the war. The lost or phantom trains of Trobitz, the content explained, ambled through a vanquished Germany for more than twenty days.

The Nazis evacuated the *Camp de l'étoile* in Bergen-Belsen on 5 April 1945, when they realized British troops were approaching. They told the *Camp de l'étoile* inmates that they would be traveling to Theresienstadt, a camp the Nazis ordered staged as a showplace in 1944 with the intention of deceiving the Red Cross into believing that Jews were happy and well treated. It was, of course, all a lie.

Gardens were planted, houses painted, and barracks renovated. There, among others, dwelled well-known Jewish artists, who put on shows and directed plays, gave concerts, wrote symphonies. They included children, who painted pictures and wrote poetry. Even so their lives were not secure. Their stay was always short; they were expendable, their days numbered, their destinations preassigned for travel to various other death camps.

More than two thousand people from the *Camp de l'étoile* were loaded on trucks. They were driven or marched to the train station that had first witnessed their arrival in Bergen-Belsen. There they climbed into dilapidated cattle trains, most of them open to the elements. Subsequently, the deportees were exposed to bombardments from the advancing allies. The Nazis abandoned their prisoners on the railroad tracks and fled; the prisoners were free, but in what shape? Many had died—most others were just barely alive. Eventually my research about Trobitz led to the memoirs of Albert Bigielman and Jacques Saurel.*

Albert and Jacques wrote of their lives as teenaged members of the *Camp de l'étoile* in Drancy, Bergen-Belsen, and Trobitz, sharing the same horrible itinerary my mother followed. I am indebted to them for publishing their painful memories of those times because their revelations constitute the last chapter of my mother's ordeals. From them I learned more about the horrific life people in Bergen-Belsen were submitted to, and I discovered what occurred on the way to Trobitz. In fact, Bigielman's memoir includes the names of 258 deportees who reached this final destination, and this list included my own mother's name, Carmen Grozinger.

The end of the war brought an improbable light to the end of the dark tunnel of imprisonment in concentration camps. After the Nazi soldiers fled, those individuals who could still walk after the harsh traveling conditions went on or were transported to Trobitz. There they found food and clothing in abandoned houses. Tragically, many, unaware that eating too much and too rapidly could kill them, passed away in these circumstances. Just as Carmen reported, a Russian commando unit, some of whom were Cossacks wearing exotic furs, rushed in like a mirage out of the desert. These were the liberators spreading panic among the last German inhabitants and the confused survivors alike.

Order was soon reestablished under the command of a capable female Russian captain, who showed kindness toward those deportees. She ordered the remaining German population to bury the dead and

---

*De Drancy à Bergen-Belsen, 1944-1945: Souvenirs rassemblés d'un enfant déporté [From Drancy to Bergen-Belsen, 1944-45] by Jacques Saurel; and *J'ai eu douze ans à Bergen-Belsen* [I Turned Twelve in Bergen-Belsen] by Albert Bigielman. Both books are published in French by La Fondation pour la Mémoire de la Shoah.

PART TWO—LILIANE
CHAPTER THIRTY-TWO

move the sick into available housing. She requisitioned food, clean clothes, and bedding. Unfortunately, the Russians carried no medicines with them. Mothers not already sick with typhus themselves received instructions to wash their children from head to toe with hot soapy water six to eight times per day to kill the lice that caused the disease. However, the Russians' main objective was to move on, to continue the war on the fleeing Nazis, not to fulfill a humanitarian mission. Before leaving, they wished to make arrangements to repatriate the surviving deportees, not through Europe, but through Russia to the detriment of the deportees. Fortunately, two officers of the French Army, ex-POWs who had regained their freedom earlier than others, heard that their families might be alive in the Russian occupation zone. They arrived with two Jeeps to take their loved ones out. These included a mother and daughter arrested by the French police while crossing over in the so-called "Free Zone." In 1942 when she was arrested, Francine Christophe was seven years old. She and her mother spent the next two years being transferred from one French detention camp to another, sometimes back and forth to the same destination; this until 1944 when they were finally transported to Bergen-Belsen. How the girl and her mother survived such a long period of deprivations and misery is nothing short of miraculous.

    I declare that all of those who died as well as those who survived the camps were heroes, my mother included. Some fought to endure pain day after day, while others like my mother helped to soothe their compatriots as long as they were able. An unwilling participant for sure, she nevertheless showed the resilience of her mind in spite of the atrophying welfare and functions of her body. Even in these debilitating conditions, she protected two motherless teenagers, who came to visit her in Paris twice after the war ended.

That's why I forgave Carmen instinctively again and again, despite her moods and sudden angers. She had suffered. Many a night I fell asleep crying about the trials and humiliations she survived.

At the war's end in Trobitz, Francine Christophe's father retrieved his wife, still delirious from the effects of typhus, and an overjoyed daughter, herself in poor health, on 6 June 1945. On that occasion Francine ran toward him as fast as her swollen legs allowed. This French officer was not in the position to take other deportees with him, but word about Trobitz was finally out.

Carmen lived to be seventy-nine, though her last decade was a nightmare. First a stroke sent her to the hospital where she stayed in intensive care for several days attached to an array of tubes. I came to visit and peered at her through what appeared to be a large incubator. It made me wish she could be a baby again, a baby with a better fate. Later, when she improved enough for surgery, her head was shaved, the blood inside her brain stanched. Once more she looked uncannily like the recent survivor of a concentration camp.

Her doctor said the prognosis for her recovery was bleak; there might be paralysis, cognitive deficits, and speech impairment, and surely problems with routine activities and chronic pain that would restrict the quality of her daily life. Carmen's doctor was right and wrong at the same time. She recovered relatively rapidly from the operation and the trauma. She walked and talked again in a rather outstandingly short period of time; her memory was intact. This stability lasted for some time, and then little by little her body began

PART TWO—LILIANE
CHAPTER THIRTY-TWO

to deteriorate. Carmen's arteries were clogged. She was losing her hearing, had difficulties walking, her sight diminished. She could not read or watch television. She made an effort to hide her pain and held up a proud face.

Then Michel called me in the middle of the night from France to say that Carmen was in a coma. Her legs were black with gangrene. I should come immediately, which I did with my uncle, Fred Time, faithful to his sister to the very end.

Chapter Thirty-Three

Fred, my favorite brother, who survived the war with me, suffered a slipped disk that left him paralyzed in one leg at age sixty, a time that coincided with his retirement. In spite of this leaden leg, with great effort and concentration he learned to shuffle along with a cane. He and Jeanette continued to travel and visit their son, daughter, and assorted grandchildren. To my surprise and delight they also came to visit their American family during the winter of 1999. On that occasion, we flew from Dallas to San Antonio to visit my daughter, Arielle, and her husband, Thad. They took us on a tour of this historic town. Fred loved the Alamo, the Missions, and the Mercado. He bought souvenirs with enthusiasm, particularly a loudly multicolored parrot piñata. Back in Dallas, he and Jeanette celebrated the New Year with my family and friends. I felt so honored, so happy to have them in my house.

"This is my brother," I told everyone proudly. Later my friend Alain said, "When you say 'my brother,' we all know you mean Fred, but when you talk about your other brothers, you call them by their names."

I visited my family in France almost yearly and was always welcome in Fred and Jeanette's home. We spent many rewarding hours there, laughed and ate, debated politics, disagreed and sometimes fought over it. But Fred and I never spoke about the war years when he and I were refugees in a village in the south of France. Now I would give anything to know the answers to the important questions I failed to ask him.

One of the questions I should have asked him touches upon the time we arrived in Sabres and were separated; Fred with one family, I with another. After he was able to visit me, I wondered, what did we talk about? Did I inquire as to why we were not living together? Did I ask about what had happened to my mother? Did he tell me anything about our parents? I would also ask him how he felt when the father he hardly remembered took him back to Paris and placed him in a semi-orphanage where he stayed until my mother returned and was strong enough to take care of him.

A year after his visit to the United States, Fred's health declined. He couldn't tell me what was wrong because he himself didn't know. His platelet count was low, and he needed frequent blood transfusions. Finally the cause was discovered. Fred suffered from an acute form of leukemia.

I spoke to people seeking help and advice, especially to Monique, my best friend and a nurse by training. She told me to prepare myself for an unhappy outcome. Two other friends, both researchers and medical doctors, confirmed her prognosis. I sobbed and cried and wept, and thought they were all wrong. I searched the Internet for hours to see if there existed some reprieve for Fred, perhaps some new medication to combat the disease. I found a medication called "Gleevec," an experimental drug that controlled some kinds of leukemia. I suggested it to a respected oncologist when I arrived in France. "No," said the doctor who agreed to talk to me, "your brother's leukemia would not benefit from the treatment, even if we had that drug."

PART TWO—LILIANE
CHAPTER THIRTY-THREE

Nothing more could be done, but I couldn't accept Fred's impending demise. When you have a brother, he remains yours for your entire life. Why was he being stolen from me? Swallowing my pride, I asked the psychologist at the high school where I taught if I could come talk to him. I was planning to visit my dying brother, I told him, but was afraid I wouldn't know what to say or how to act.

"Be yourself. That's certainly what your brother would expect from you," Dr. George said. It would be hard to be myself. What good would it do for him to see my sorrow?

I got a substitute and made ready to go spend two weeks with Fred, first stopping in Paris to pick up my ninety-one-year-old father, who would voyage with me by train.

A parent never expects to outlive his children. My father hid his grief the only way he knew—by acting rational. There was a cause to Fred's disease, he reasoned; he had done too much sport during his life. He clung to this explanation. He repeated it like a mantra.

"I kept telling him to stop doing all these sports. Did he need to take judo in middle age? He made something slip inside his body. He was excessive; he would not listen to me. He always did things like that."

"When Fred was fifteen he decided he wanted to be a cyclist. He measured his thighs; they were the same size as Géminiani's, his hero, the winner of the Tour de France. I tried to dissuade him, but no, he was going to do Paris to Brussels and back with a friend in six days. He did it, but came back more dead than alive, and slept for forty-eight hours."

I understood what my father was trying to say. Like the rest of the family, he was aware that Fred's disease was a form of cancer, an unruly bunch of cells out of control, overtaking his body. His argument was not with his son, but with death. Death could be summoned by a careless act, ergo his son must have been careless.

"One is responsible for one's actions. You have no one but yourself to blame." This is what my beloved father told me when I cried after touching the snow in Paris. Snow was a rarity in Sabres. I was not used to it. Sternly, he forbade my crying. Indeed, I was so startled by his attitude that I immediately stopped. It was not the snow's fault but my own if my hands felt stung and numb. After much deliberating on my part, I accepted my father's premise as truth, and him as my mentor.

These exhortations were the tools he handed us to cope with life. Indeed his own had been like an ocean filled with waves that tossed him here and there. His wife had already died. Yet, I found his faith in his capacities to act and mitigate the vagaries of life entirely admirable. They were kicking in again to help him cope with his son's impending death.

We arrived at the hospital, a sad, depressing place of peeling hallways and floors that smelled like Clorox, and found Fred chatting with his roommate. I was happily surprised. My brother seemed lively. As was his wont, he told jokes, and we laughed salutarily. He got up to go to the restroom, a feat that provoked my father and I to exchange looks shining with glimmers of hope. His therapist came in to massage his legs.

"When I am well again and can go home and exercise, will I regain the muscles in my legs?" Fred asked her.

"Of course," she replied.

We listened, awestruck. Was there something we hadn't been

PART TWO—LILIANE
CHAPTER THIRTY-THREE

told? Perhaps Fred wasn't quite aware of the gravity of his situation. Or did he have a chance to survive this killer cancer for a much longer period of time?

Looking back, I realize that Fred acted and spoke as he did to protect us, so we wouldn't feel sad right away. He laughed and joked with us as long as he could. This is what I want to believe, for otherwise he had clung to hope and saw it diminish, literally day by day. Five days after I arrived he was no longer able to get up unassisted; a couple days later he was completely bedbound. He was pale, and he hurt. He was given morphine around the clock and slept most of the time. When he emerged from his deep sleep, he looked up and saw us encircling him. We smiled, touched his forehead, kissed his cheeks, squeezed his arms, letting him know we were there with him.

Then came the day I had to say goodbye.

"Will you be back?" he asked wearily.

"Of course, very soon," I said, holding back my tears. I leaned over him, hugged him and murmured, "I love you, I've always loved you," realizing it was the first time ever I had told him so.

Fred died in great pain two weeks later. I thought I would not go to his funeral, perhaps because I had not been able to keep my promise to come and see him again, but I did go for the rest of my family, for the sense of communion that binds us.

Months later on the telephone, I asked Jeannette if she knew whether Fred understood how much I loved him. "You bet. He always knew how much his little sister loved him, and he loved her back with all his heart and soul," she assured me.

My Fred, I meet you in my dreams. You are in my life forever.

Chapter Thirty-Four

Many years after both my parents passed away, my brother Michel brought me an ordinary, lidless carton box and asked me to look through the papers and photographs it contained. In it I found the letters Eugène sent to Carmen, first to Drancy and then to Bergen-Belsen. They were creased, folded in two, yellowed by time. The messages were brief because the official space for correspondence, more postcard size than letter, was so restricted. I gave them the once-over, put them away in an envelope, and forgot about them.

It was only when I began writing this memoir about my family that I remembered the postcards. This second look unearthed a trove of information that I had missed and brought up a critical question. How did my mother manage to save those stained papers and bring them back with her? I realized with a shock that my mother must have carried them from Drancy to Bergen-Belsen and, finally, to Trobitz, where she had lain in a coma induced by typhus at the end of a brutal odyssey.

Of course all communications were monitored during the war. Words were carefully chosen. Eugène's first letter mentions the children—but not where they are—and describes his emotions—"I am sad, so sad"—regarding Carmen's detention at Drancy. It had been a month since he had heard anything directly from her. Since there was no room to expand on thoughts and feelings, the tone of the message seems awkward, even somewhat detached. It mirrors the situation, the separation, the lack of significant words; but not necessarily the true sentiments the sender and the recipient must have felt when they read the contents. The second letter also contains news about the children. Expressions of Eugène's growing concern for Carmen can be intuited in the too-brief message.

These are stamped with the name of the Austrian prison camp where my father and his fellow prisoners of many nationalities were detained.

I imagine my mother reading and rereading these brief messages during her terrible ordeal, protecting them against the somber odds. The notes represented a wager of her identity, of her connection to the outside world, and of her membership in a family who loved her—all this was evidence of the very beliefs the Nazis endeavored to destroy in their victims. My mother preserved them during the worst of circumstances. Those nursing her in Trobitz, while she struggled with dysentery and typhus, probably found the postcards hidden within her tattered clothes and returned them to her when her quarantine ended. She brought them back with her after her liberation and kept them as long as she lived.

The very notion that mail was delivered in some parts of Bergen-Belsen also strikes me as absurd. Mail seems too civilized a concept to fit in that world of calculated deprivation. But the Nazis thought about everything; in this instance, they gave with the one hand to better take away with the other. The forced brevity and censure of contents deprived the correspondents of the information they longed to hear. "How are you? I love you. The children are well. So

PART TWO—LILIANE
CHAPTER THIRTY-FOUR

and so wrote to me. I got a package." Mail from a loved one in any kind of shape remained a bittersweet solace for the inmate; so much had to stay unsaid.

Once Carmen told us a story she had never told before. The families of wives and children of prisoners of war lived in an enclave of Bergen-Belsen called *Camp de l'étoile*, so-called because they arrived with clothes bearing yellow stars. Wives of prisoners of war were valuable; they could be traded for German POWs. It was a dubious pretext. No one was ever exchanged. To carry on the charade, these women were spared the branding of numbers on their arms.

However, this status coupled with her native command of German gave Carmen a slight advantage. On one occasion, she related, she asked the German commandant in charge of their unit for pen, paper and stamps.

"Imagine your wife were in my position," she told him. "Wouldn't you be happy to receive a letter from her? I am like your wife, a woman who loves her husband, and who, thanks to you, will be able to communicate with him."

He was stunned by the tone of her voice, and luckily for her did not retaliate in any violent way. Moreover, incredibly, he procured the asked for necessities. This could only have happened at the beginning of Carmen's incarceration, for afterward things fell apart, due to the increasing arrival of new detainees and to the hellish conditions of the camp.

No letters from Carmen to Eugène survived. He had been moved around from one place to another so many times he might have lost them. She clung to hers, and they became a presence, a proof that someone in this dark world cared about her and waited for her return.

Even so, in spite of the hundreds of books written by survivors, and the many movies that have dealt with this subject matter and continue to appear, I find it impossible to imagine the daily miseries Carmen and others endured. I could never have survived the proximity and the promiscuity of concentration camp life, the noises, the odious smells of the latrines, the lice, the absence of food, the lack of medical care, the senseless persecutions, and in the end, the debilitating and deadly diseases.

Witnesses corroborated everything that my mother told us during the course of our upbringing. They related the dreary routines of work detail, of endless calls to line up in whatever weather conditions, to be counted and recounted, a process that could go on for hours. They recalled the incessant hunger and cold, the never-won battles with lice that devoured the prisoners slowly. They told about the daily deaths of people, so commonplace that the deportees did not take time to mourn individuals, even those who had been their friends. Toward the end of the war it was not unusual to step on bodies, they had become a familiar landscape.

Carmen rarely mentioned the slave labor she and her companions were forced to do. They were assigned the task of transporting huge cauldrons filled with boiling water; a backbreaking job for these frail, underfed women arriving at their destination already exhausted. Their job involved plunging their bare hands into the vessels to retrieve and empty the silk cocoons they contained, an operation constituting one more unbearable torture.

"Dirty, painful work," my mother used to say, shaking her head in disbelief.

But growing up, my brothers and I knew next to nothing about

PART TWO—LILIANE
CHAPTER THIRTY-FOUR

Carmen's daily life in that place. She only admitted to small details, such as never abandoning care of her body, in spite of the long lines of people waiting their turn at the few faucets that ran with frigid water. At times the weather itself was punishing, and the water turned to ice. Then she would use some of her precious drinking water to cleanse herself.

This information made us cringe. We did not know what to say. We were afraid to probe and yet still wondered. Did she not have soap, a toothbrush, and what about toothpaste? Privately, I imagined her in a Hieronymus Bosch hell inhabited by hundreds of tortured human beings dying in terrible pain, a tableau apparently not far from the truth.

In the end, my mother could not share many particulars of the world of horrors she had experienced and endured. She observed a kind of severe restraint about these matters, which separated her from her family. Even after the revelations of witnesses testifying at Eichmann's trial, Carmen remained quiet, having decided once and for all to carry the baggage of that past by herself.

The Eichmann trial in 1961-62 stunned its global audience. The prosecutors graphically described the ever-evolving imaginative cruelty used by the Nazis in their zeal to torture and annihilate Jews and other groups, including people with disabilities, Romish, Polish, Christians deemed a threat, and too many others, who must not be forgotten. Eichmann, who held in his hands the fates of thousands of innocent people, defended himself of any culpability in the matter of their annihilation with a famous scant unforgettable sentence: "I was only a cog in a machine." Does a cog have a brain, a heart, and a natural empathy toward fellow human beings?

Can we conclude that Eichmann therefore was not a human being? And yet he was, and I admit I cheered when I heard the verdict against him: guilty of crimes against humanity, condemned to death by hanging.

I imagined what Carmen would write to me in a letter if she could have found the words.

Dear Liliane,

I pawned my good jewelry to buy salamis on the black market so your father would have something to eat. He was a prisoner of war. I was told I might be able to see him before he was sent to prison camp in Germany.

There I was, eight months pregnant with you, traveling half a day on the train by myself. When I arrived, everything looked gray and cold. I walked all the way to the barbed wire gate with my package. The guard said that what was left of the regiment had left the night before. I cried my eyes out and took the train back to Paris.

Before the war, your father and I would go for walks at night in the city. We watched the sky and the glittering stars. When the conquerors took Paris and began testing their racial theories of unequal rights, they made us wear yellow stars.

When my time came, your brother and I walked to Hôtel-Dieu Hospital. Tack, tack, tack, the sound of bombs accompanied us. But you were perfect and beautiful, and for a few

PART TWO—LILIANE
CHAPTER THIRTY-FOUR

moments, I forgot we were alone in the middle of a war. Then I sent you and your brother away, not knowing when or if I'd ever see you again.

The Gestapo and the French police came for me at five in the morning. Because I was a Jew, they herded me into a bus already filled with other women and children. That was the bus your father and I took to go to the stadium to cheer our soccer team. Those were exciting times. But now for me, only gloom. I was taken to Drancy, then shipped like cattle to Bergen-Belsen where death hovered like an annoying, tireless fly. I called for death daily. Yet, after many months, typhus, dysentery, quarantine, and liberation, I came home, a skeleton on two canes. We were reunited, but no longer knew one another. I may seem hard and unloving at times but please try to understand. My heart has trouble beating by itself; the blood doesn't flow well through my arteries. Forgive me. Someday, I will tell you everything.

Love, Carmen

Chapter Thirty-Five

Eugène grieved quietly for his wife of fifty years but could not repress forever his talent for enjoying life. He continued discovering events and situations and enthusiastically told us about them.

"I never realized that these transsexuals suffered so much," he told me during my annual visit as he turned off the television set.

"Imagine that, wanting to be a different sex. It must involve lots of pain to have yourself transformed from male to female or vice versa. I can't believe it's even possible. As for myself, even thinking about wearing high heels or putting stockings on makes me cringe. All the same, I think these individuals have lots of courage."

I was awed to hear my father speak that freely about sex changes. Sex had never been a topic in our household. My father and my mother both were ultra secretive about anything concerning these particular physiological features. Words like "breast" or "penis" did not exist in our vocabulary. At fifteen, I didn't know what sex was about, though one day a school friend tried to enlighten me. What she said seemed gross, and I rejected the idea. And then I got my first period, an event my mother whispered in my father's ear as soon as he came home from work. He responded with a groan. I overheard and was embarrassed. I remember turning red with the heat of shame thinking to myself that, though unwillingly, I had done something really wrong. At last I got my courage up and asked my mother to explain what was happening to me.

"This is a woman's burden, you'll have to get used to it," she replied; and that was that.

During his last years my father went on living, singing in the morning, eating with relish, listening to the radio, rereading all his books, discussing politics, and talking, talking, talking about everything, helped in those tasks by a woman thirty years younger than he, who loved and respected him.

Fred, Michel, and I were happy he had found a partner. Without an interlocutor, someone interested in what he said, who answered and asked questions, he would have literally, as well as figuratively died of boredom. I believe that my mother would have approved the relationship, would have been happy that someone was taking care of her husband. Monique never tired of hearing Eugène talk about his childhood. His mother's ghost often visited the stories. In his very last years he questioned why he had been separated from her at an early age. As the years passed and Eugène reached his nineties, he complained about being old. Age was robbing him of too many of the pleasures of life, he said. He was adamant he'd rather not celebrate any more birthdays.

"Save your money. I don't need any presents. I already have too many things that I need to throw out," he complained.

"Good," said Fred, who collected all kinds of antiques. "Then you can begin with that old stove in the corner of the living room. I've had an eye on it for quite some time."

PART TWO—LILIANE
CHAPTER THIRTY-FIVE

"That piece of junk! Pèpère gave it to your mother. I don't know why she liked it so much. Take it."

"And what about that book I've been asking you to lend me?"

"Sorry," responded my father. "If I loaned it to you you'd keep it. It belongs to my library, I cannot part with it."

We teased him; there were things he was still passionate about. He laughed and we laughed. We were happy to be together. Monique served her famous apple pie, and life together tasted as good as ever.

And then Fred died. My father buried him, as we all did, with much sorrow and bitter tears. What parent wants their child to die before him? Yet Eugène survived surrounded by the living and the events of the world.

I have this image of my father walking slowly but proudly erect without a cane to the grocery store where he and Monique always found something to shop for. The last morning of his life he was dressed, waiting for Monique, who was taking her shower. As he bent down to put his shoes on, death snatched him. He had no time to think and did not suffer. A sudden heart attack ended his life at age ninety-four.

This best-of-raconteurs lived as fully as he could even during the worse of circumstances. He watched a movie on television the evening preceding his death and ate some chocolate to round out a meal that was always to his taste. I shed no tears at the funeral. He had endured no lingering sickness and had never been bedridden.

My mother, my father, my brother, Papa and Maman Dublanc, Mamée and Papé, dear departed, still alive in the universe, forever revolving in my mind.

Epilogue

My parents' experiences of the war overshadowed my childhood and my adolescence. They became the reference with which I measured the course of my life. I knew I had been saved from death. The worse thing that could happen to me would always be insignificant when compared with the degree of miseries Carmen and Eugène endured.

My elbow was shattered when I was in high school. I received penicillin shots twice a day for the next six months and missed a lot of school in the process, but I consoled myself. I wasn't in Drancy or in Bergen-Belsen; death did not hover around me. I would recover, go to Sabres again, and return to Paris as always. This rationale became a mediating mechanism. It helped me manage the vexations of life. I had clothes and food, considered everything a gift—the rain and the gray days as well as the sunny ones. I truly believed myself to be the luckiest person in the world.

During the trial of Adolf Eichmann in the early 1960s, I discovered the full history of the Holocaust in all its stupefying savagery. I became a witness myself, watching the televised testimony of survivors, who described the tortures and murders of millions of people. Those emaciated faces, those tortured bones are part of my psyche. I honor their memories as I think about them.

Around this time, after my high school graduation, I came to the United States to meet my grandparents, cousins, aunts, and uncles. Though I had not intended to leave France permanently, I met a good-looking young man in Dallas, Texas, and we were married four months after my arrival. All was well, but I missed my family and France. I was not working and got bored. And then one day my uncle Fred gave me a suggestion, "Why don't you go to college?"

I duly received a B.A, after that an M.A, and began teaching high school. By then, two wonderful children were part of our lives. Later on, I decided I would return to the university. This time I chose a field of study encompassing history, film, and aesthetics taught in the newly established "History of Ideas" department at the University of Texas. I knew the focus of my study would deal with war. It took me four years to complete my coursework and two more to write my dissertation. My scholarly endeavor aimed to stage, speak about, and represent the struggles of the human spirit in its attempts to endow with meaning, affirm, recreate, refute, or reject the circumstances of time and place. I dedicated *Themes and Ideology in the Vietnam Films 1975-1983* to Carmen, Eugène, and Fred.

A Tour Through The Gardens

Seed of women seed of men
Good seeds bad seeds
There was
Always a garden

Little girl lucky me
Into the world at war
Sent to safety on a rattling train
Held and soothed
By darling brother Fred
Magically transported
To a village surrounded by forests
Pungent sap of tall pines
Harvested for the making of turpentine
Carpet of ferns curly loves tight as fists
Covering the ground for miles
And the pure air
Lungs of the Landes forest
Inhaled far from bombs and ashes

THE BONES OF TIME

Sometimes my foster mother
And Paulette take me with them to church
For Pentecost I wear a big white ribbon in my hair
And Fred is a choirboy
But I don't remember my real mother
Coming south to see us
Shortly before they round her up in Paris
And send her to Drancy and Bergen-Belsen
For the next three years

Perhaps what I do remember
So one afternoon
In my foster parents' home
The bent knee of a helmeted occupier
Offering me candy
But all in all life goes on merrily for me
Child whose earlier memories
Are already erased

I go to the one schoolroom
Learn to read and count with sticks
Play under an upturned chair
My stage

And there is always Fred
Who lodges with another family
And no longer hides behind bushes
To visit with me

A TOUR THROUGH THE GARDENS

From age three to six then
Nary a fear except from fairy tales
A thrill safely vented
Under the watch of seraphim
Hovering in a semicircle
Above the fireplace

My major household god is Paulette
Redoubtable on her elephantine legs
How I loved her and still do
Who cured me of mange
Potty-trained me authoritatively
And took me for rides
On the back of her bicycle
Warning sternly
Keep your feet away
From the spokes

In the village we buy bread
For an entire week
Gossip with everyone
I love the dentist Pierre Chaulet
Make him swear to marry me when I grow up
And how in awe of Monsieur Turok I am
The deaf and dumb man
Who grunts amiably and kisses my hand
Chivalrously

THE BONES OF TIME

Viens faire un tour de jardin
A spin a farandole a cabriole
At the end of summer afternoons
Come along! Let's take a look at the garden
Suggests Paulette
We put on espadrilles and leave the big house
Wealthy well-appointed filled with ancient toys
Postcards books silver coins
Apples duvets hand-embroidered linens
Homemade preserves
In armoires

And traverse the road watching for oncoming traffic
Stopping midway near Jesus' cross twenty feet above us
Safely to the other side we reach a narrow path
Lined with brambles
Leading to the gleaming garden
Porous gray soil
Matrix of strawberries tomatoes onions cabbages and potatoes
Thriving under the sun

Where did this universe stop when it did I wondered
With a fence around the earth girding it
A security belt preventing humans from slipping
And disappearing in whatever lay beyond it

A TOUR THROUGH THE GARDENS

And all around the garden
Where water sprung from an old pump
Stretched prairies where cows with first names
Untagged unhampered grazed in the field
And knew time
Returning with measured steps to stables at dusk
Their bells echoing through the air
Making me believe the entire world always
Held such peace

Then I left paradise
That first meeting in Paris with my real family
Strange father strange broken mother
A new baby brother
Only familiar Fred big brother always my favorite
Every one but he strangers nevertheless reunited
Struggling to get on our feet in a two and a half room apartment
And yet dreams spun for hours
In a space like a small closet
The communal toilet shared by three families
A hole in a recess with two steps for the feet
Through its small window
I saw rooftops through clouds
And there read future fame

THE BONES OF TIME

Just two short streets away
From our rue des Francs Bourgeois apartment
A significant garden opened up its vista
A large public square with buildings on four sides
Bricked in red and white
Like fancy bonbons
Surrounded by arcades
Place des Vosges where I grew up
Where my mother brothers and I
Came for relaxation Wednesdays and Saturdays
Sometime we fought there then made friends
And Fred played soccer fervidly until dark
When our exasperated father came to get him by the ear

In the middle of the park stands an equestrian statue
With a Louis the umpteenth regal in the saddle
Staring across the street
Towards Victor Hugo's residence
Where Gavroche Colette and Jean Valjean
Were conceived

Once a poetry fair took place in Place des Vosges
Paul Fort was crowned Prince of Poets
It was my first time breathing the air of the literati
Another time my mother seated on a park chair
Glanced up and saw a handsome soldier
In American uniform

A TOUR THROUGH THE GARDENS

Looked hard at him and after a moment
Burst into tears
Recognizing the brother she had last seen
As a young boy

Mon oncle d'Amérique
Whose bride-to-be had a brother
Which is how I come to be in my present garden
On the other side of the Atlantic
In the far reaches of Texas
In Dallas where J.F.K was shot
In the budding flower of his age

And in my own garden
Like Louis XIV
Deciding what for each season
And where to put it
A stone path an arbor a bench
Sculptures around a bend
Also a vegetable garden
Lush with promises in early spring
Most shriveling at June's end in this harsh hot climate

But in winter
I like how everything dies to the ground
As if it had never existed
And how the same

THE BONES OF TIME

Surprises in spring
Faithful perennials and flowering trees
As lovely as when first planted

While those who have disappeared
Folded inside my heart
Tight spores
As real as photographs
Seeds of memories
From beginning to end

Acknowledgements

This memoir has taken generations and has spanned continents to write. It began in a place that I will never visit, in a time well before my birth; hopefully it will be carried in the future to places I do not know how to imagine, long after I am gone. Because this is my wish, I want to thank my grandchildren, Adrian and Eliane Spalding, in advance for reading it and giving it to their children, and their children's children. In this way do the bones of time remain fleshed.

I want to thank the following people for their contributions to my story and its publication: Eugène Grozinger for his love and attention, his endurance and cynicism, and his zeal for film and discourse; Carmen Tieme Grozinger for surviving and persisting, for giving me life, for her courage and sense, for all that she was; my beloved brother Fred for watching over me and protecting me when I was too small to protect myself, for a great love and kinship, and for starting me on this journey by taking the first steps. I am grateful for my brothers Michel and Patrick, who were and are part of my growth and evolution. Thank you to my faithful uncle, my mother's brother, Fred Elias Time, who has supported me, made me laugh, accompanied me by foot, bicycle, car, plane, and boat, and has sung with me for more than six decades. I also owe an eternal debt of gratitude to the Dublanc family not only for taking me in as their own, but also for loving me and giving me an idyllic childhood. In a time of fear, pain, and devastation, I have memories of beauty and affection, red geraniums in pots upon the windowsills, and crisp lace curtains blowing on the breeze. Thank you to Paulette Dublanc for still receiving me with warmth.

Thank you to my early readers, David Delambre, Edie Brickell, and Christina Morris, for their close attention and valuable commentary, and to Deborah Reardon who encouraged me and lifted my spirits when I was unsure and frustrated. Thank you to Stuart Younse who gave me an opportunity to present my story to an audience I would not have otherwise encountered, in a manner I would not have foreseen.

Thank you to Maribeth Lipscomb for making herself available whenever I asked, for her willingness and patience, and for her technical support. A special thanks to Sarah Theobald-Hall, my editor, for making me read my words through new eyes, for her awareness and exactitude, for her gentle relentlessness in the pursuit of the authentic and genuine, and, of course, for her friendship. I would be remiss if I did not also thank Jill K. Sayre for bringing Sarah and I together. Laura Gloege read what I had written, rearranged it, and made it better. Thank you to Susan Falk for her proofreading skills and enthusiasm.

Last but not least, thank you to Ted Ruybal at Wisdom House Books, who designed the book and the gorgeous covers.

I would like to thank my husband, Harvey Richman, who has always supported my writing. He has read my work honestly and critically and is unfailingly encouraging. Finally, a heartfelt thank you to my daughters, Adina and Arielle who have toiled to respect and revise *Bones of Time*, and lastly to my son-in-law, Thad Spalding—they are all my helpmates and my inspiration.

CPSIA information can be obtained
at www.ICGtesting.com
Printed in the USA
FSOW01n2359280316
18420FS